ORGANIZATION
AND MANAGEMENT
IN SCHOOLS
perspectives for practising teachers

Alan Paisey

Longman
London and New York

To Mark and Timothy

Longman Group UK Limited
Longman House, Burnt Mill, Harlow
Essex CM20 2JE, England
and Associated Companies throughout the world

Published in the United States of America
by Longman Inc., New York

© Longman Group Limited 1981

First published 1981
Second impression 1983
Third impression 1985
Fourth impression 1987

British Library Cataloguing in Publication Data

Paisey, Alan
  Organization and management in schools.
  1. School management and organization –
  Great Britain
  I. Title
  371.2'00941   LB2901   80–41165

ISBN 0-582-49709-4

Produced by Longman Singapore Publishers (Pte) Ltd.
Printed in Singapore.

CONTENTS

PREFACE

In the management of organizations, the beginning of wisdom is to recognize that there is no single and irrefutable formula to be learned and applied. Knowledge of a general nature is involved, including the wide range of theories derived from the experience of others. Personal skills of many kinds are involved, including those which may be acquired by imitation or by deliberate study away from the job. In the end, however, management is a practical activity, undertaken for real purposes with real people. It has specific aspects, therefore, involving particular knowledge, singular personalities and local variations of principle, custom and purpose. There is always a unique flavour – though varied in strength – to the management of every school.

From this premise it may be asserted that there is no *one* way to manage a school, only that management is always partly subjective, partly objective; partly concerned with values, partly concerned with facts; partly a matter of intuition, partly a matter of measurement.

This book is intended to help teachers in their task of managing schools as efficiently and as effectively as possible. For those who are already in senior positions or who are heads of schools, it attempts to offer conceptual clarification based on an 'organizational behaviour' approach. For those who aspire to such positions it offers in addition an indication of the scope, scale and nature of the work which goes into managing the school.

School management is concerned with all the human activity which makes up the school as an ongoing organization. The school as an organization is maintained to keep open activities devoted to learning. Schools are managed by teachers who normally make their way by progressive stages in their careers from straightforward responsibilities for teaching a prescribed group or number of groups of pupils to becoming the head of the entire organization. Managerial capacity in the teacher is less an optional extra which *some* teachers ought to have, more a necessary part of the professional qualification and achievement of every teacher.

As may be seen from the following quotation, all teachers may play some part in the management of their schools but heads of schools and other senior staff face formal and inescapable responsibilities for the management of the school. In talking about management

> we are addressing the interests and responsibilities of all who have a significant part to play in the functioning of organisations, viewed as groups of people who have come together in an organised way for certain purposes which those involved find reasonably compatible. We are concerned with the primary managerial functions of ensuring the optimum use of resources, determining the direction and adaptability of an organisation in a changing environment and relating aims and impact to society. A managerial role usually means being in the middle of a complex set of pressures, from within and from without, playing a part of some significance in decisions, having a share of the responsibility not only for one's own work but for that of others, and contributing towards the achievement of an often precarious balance, through influencing aims, policies and activities (Brodie 1979: 1).

Schools are sufficiently distinctive as organizations to be treated as a single, inclusive category. However, the real differences between the sectors – primary and secondary – and differences between types of school within each sector are recognized in the text in terms of conceptual consideration and illustrative material. There yet remains more to unite all schools – for the most part – as a species of public sector organizations than there is to separate them. Consequently, this book draws on the universal literature in organization theory and management studies, the general literature in education and the specific literature on primary and secondary schools.

Attention is drawn to the preference for spelling the word 'organization' throughout with a 'z', except in quotations from authors who preferred to use 's'. The word 'pupil' is used in accord with English custom for young people at school, rather than the word 'student', in accord with American custom. 'Student' is reserved for those who have entered higher education after eighteen years of age. Following the publication of the 'Taylor Report' (Department of Education and Science 1977a), the word 'governors' is used in both primary and secondary education for the body of appointed and *ex officio* people who represent the public interest in the management of each school. This term supersedes the term 'managers' which has customarily been used in the primary sector.

Chapter 1 is introductory, dealing with the nature of organization in general and the school in particular. Chapter 2 is concerned with the kind of task which the school as an organization undertakes, and Chapter 3 with the special kind of 'know-how' required to discharge it. Chapter 4 is a study of the structure of organization in schools. Chapter 5 focuses on the need for management to be effective and suggests factors which should be taken into account in trying to achieve this. Chapter 6, the final chapter, on viewpoints and values, is a consideration of the different ways in which teachers think about their schools as organizations.

I am variously indebted to a very long list of professional colleagues and acquaintances in the advisory services, schools, teachers' centres, institutions in higher education and other bodies of the counties of Berkshire and Hampshire and Oxfordshire in particular. Many other sources of inspiration and information in the United Kingdom and the United States in addition, however, would be included in the list. The names of those who have made material directly available for me to use have been included in the text in the appropriate places.

A special note of thanks must be recorded to my wife, Audrey Paisey, whose substantial experience in teaching, teacher education and educational management enabled her to offer critical and valuable suggestions in the development of the book. Its remaining inadequacies are mine. Finally, I wish to record my thanks to Pat Richards for her painstaking secretarial help.

Alan Paisey
Nettlebed, Oxon.
June, 1980

LIST OF FIGURES

LIST OF TABLES

ACKNOWLEDGEMENTS

We are grateful to the following for permission to reproduce copyright material:

Advisory Centre for Education (ACE) Ltd. for our table 2.4 adapted from p. 5 of *Where* 124, January 1977 by C. Jarman; Associated Kent Newspapers Ltd. for extracts from *Isle of Thanet Gazette*, 1980; Royal County of Berkshire Education Authority for an extract from p. 2 of *Rules of Management/Articles of Government*; The author, B. S. Bloom for an extract from his article 'The new direction in education research-alterable variables' in *Phi Delta Kappan*, Vol. 61, 6 February 1980; British Educational Administration Society and the authors for an extract from the article 'Where does self belong in the study of organizations?' by T. B. Greenfield in *Educational Administration* Vol. 6, No. 1, B.E.A.S. 1978, extract from the article 'Comparison between types of Institution in an L.E.A.' by B. Taylor in *Participation, Accountability and Decision-Making at Institutional Level* edited by Andrews and Parkes, B.E.A.S. 1974 and an extract from the article 'A Head of His Time' by G. E. Wheeler in *College Management Readings And Cases*, Vol. 1 edited by D. D. Simmons, Coombe Lodge 1971; The author, M. B. Brodie for extracts from his working paper 'Teachers – Reluctant Managers?' for the Thames Valley Regional Management Centre, 1979 (awaiting publication in amended form); The author, Tyrrell Burgess for an extract from his article 'Ways To Learn' in the *Journal of the Association of Colleges Implementing Diploma In Higher Education Programmes*; Councils and Education Press (a subsidiary of Longman Group Ltd.) for extract from *Education*; The Headmaster, Cranborne County Middle School, Dorset for an extract from a *Staff Handbook*; The author, B. Cooper for his letter to *The Daily Telegraph*, 19 May 1979; The Daily Telegraph Ltd. for extracts from the articles 'Teachers May Learn Their Own Lesson' in *The Daily Telegraph*, 19 May 1979, 'School Politics To Go', and 'Heads Back A Ban On Strikes' in *The Daily Telegraph*, 29 May 1979; The author, J. Dunham for an extract from *Organizational Stress in Schools*, 1979. Reprinted by kind permission; Emmbrook County Junior School, Wokingham for information about external activities; Forum for an extract from the article 'A century of regression' by P. Meredith in

Forum, Vol. 16, No. 2; The Foundation For Management Education and the author, N. Foy for an extract from *The Missing Links: British Management Education In The Eighties*; The Headmaster, The Greneway School for an extract from *Handbook For Parents*, 1974; Hampshire Education Authority and J. Killick for extracts from *Primary Heads In Hants* and an extract from p. 23 of *Instruments and Articles of Government*, 1976; The Henley Standard for extracts from articles in *The Henley Standard*, 6 April, 20 July, 24 August and 14 December 1979; The Controller of Her Majesty's Stationery Office for extracts from *Circular 10/65*, *Aspects of Secondary Education In England* (1979), *Ten Good Schools* (1977) and our table 4.4 adapted from tables in *Curriculum 11–16* (1977), all issued by the Department of Education and Science; International Labour Office for extracts from *Work Study*, 1964 (3rd Edition), pp. 26, 38 and 101–2, © 1979 International Labour Organisation, Geneva; The Headmaster, Langley County Secondary School, Berkshire for extracts from *Handbook For Parents*; London Express News And Feature Services for an extract from the article ' "Sex In Public" Lovers Jailed' in the *Sun* Newspaper, 13 July 1979; McGraw-Hill Book Company for our table 2.3 from *The Management of Organizations* by H. G. Hicks and C. R. Gullett, Copyright 1976; National Union of Teachers for extracts from *Teacher Participation – An Executive Report*, 1973; Oxfordshire Education Authority for extracts from *Starting Points In Self-Evaluation*; Phi Delta Kappa and the authors for an extract from the article 'Classroom stress and teacher burnout' by D. Walsh from *Phi Delta Kappan*, Vol. 61, 4 December 1979 © 1979 by Phi Delta Kappa, Inc., an extract from the article 'How to recognise a good school' by N. Postman and C. Weingartner from *Phi Delta Kappan*, 1973 © 1973 by The Phi Delta Kappa Educational Foundation, and a table of titles from *Educational Goals*, © by Phi Delta Kappa Inc.; The Reading Newspaper Company Ltd. for extracts from *Henley Mercury*, 14 June 1979 and extracts from *Reading Chronicle*, 13 and 20 July 1979. Reprinted by courtesy of Reading Chronicle and Henley Mercury; The Warden, St. Edward's School, Oxford for an extract from *Development Appeal*, 1979; Times Newspapers Ltd. for extracts from articles in *The Times, Educational Supplement*, 1974: by J. Vaizey (26 February), A. G. Watts (8 March), S. MacLure (26 July) and A. Clegg (11 October).

Whilst every effort has been made to trace the owners of copyright material, in a few cases this has proved impossible and we take this opportunity to offer our apologies to any copyright holders whose rights we may have unwittingly infringed.

I
LOOKING AT SCHOOLS AS ORGANIZATIONS

Introduction

Schools are not easy places to run. They are the scene of potential controversy between conflicting interests in society. They consist of large numbers of young people whose views, habits and behaviour are very varied and may reflect a sample of the full range of interests and conduct found in the wider community. The teaching staff often hold differing views and expect to be able to have considerable autonomy on the basis of professional qualification and standing. To bring a school to the point of being a harmonious and purposeful collective enterprise is a difficult feat of leadership and organizational ability.

Time and resources in all organizations are always subject to alternative uses, making it difficult but necessary to achieve an optimum deployment and use of staff, accommodation, finance, materials and equipment. Teaching, therefore, involves a great deal more than being accomplished as an instructor and being able to enforce orderly behaviour. It requires a capacity for management. Such a capacity is a necessary part of the professional standing and qualification of the teacher. Without it, teachers may not only fall short of being able to manage the school successfully, but suffer personal strain and, perhaps, failure. The following *verbatim* quotation from a letter written by a deputy-head teacher (dated 20 November 1979) illustrates the need for teachers to have managerial competence and confidence, particularly at senior level:

> School life isn't what it used to be, in fact it can be almost
> intolerable, yet we're not trained to do any other job, and nowadays
> you do need two salaries. I expect ... told you I have given up my
> Deputy Head's job and got a transfer after $2^1/_2$ years with the new
> head. I was the 6th to go, and another left this summer – even the
> marvellous caretaker who has been there about 20 odd years is
> leaving at Xmas – he can't stand her any longer. Ah well, the only
> thing to do is to get away; you can't win – Heads seem inviolate.
> I'm ever so happy in my school at ... and am Acting Deputy there
> this term until they appoint. I shan't apply – I never want to be in
> that position again! Besides, they seem to be appointing youngsters

now, late 20s – early 30s. They'll be stuck with them for a long
time!

Definitions in education

There is considerable justification for the fact that confusion reigns in the
mind of teachers over the concept of management. A number of different
but related words and phrases are in widespread use. They are either
ambiguous or seem to be similar to one another. Probably the most
frequently used and the most ambiguous word in the teacher's
vocabulary is that of 'education' itself. The term 'management' clearly
brings further ambiguity to that vocabulary. The situation is
compounded by the additional use of two phrases derived from these two
words – 'management education' and 'educational management'.

'Education' and 'management' are large and complex concepts.
Many definitions of each may be found in the respective bodies of
international literature available for students in these fields of study. It is
clear that no single definition in either field commands the unreserved
acceptance of all. It is necessary to reduce ambiguity as far as possible,
however, even though precision cannot be achieved in such studies,
which essentially lack the characteristics of exact sciences. Hence, for the
practical purposes of writing this book a number of working definitions
have been borne in mind. These are offered as an indication of the critical
distinctions between education, management and the two important
derivations which are in common use today. They provide a basis for
thinking about the management of a school as an organization and the
education of young people which schools are intended to provide.

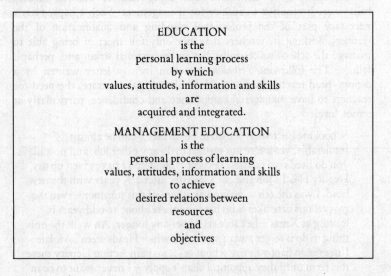

```
                    EDUCATION
                       is the
              personal learning process
                      by which
      values, attitudes, information and skills
                         are
               acquired and integrated.

              MANAGEMENT EDUCATION
                       is the
              personal process of learning
      values, attitudes, information and skills
                    to achieve
              desired relations between
                      resources
                         and
                     objectives
```

In behavioural terms it may be seen from these definitions that 'education' and 'management education' are personal experiences which imply changes in the individual concerned. Other people may certainly be involved in various capacities to facilitate and promote such experiences. In the final analysis, however, the individual decides how receptive he or she will be to what is offered and what use is made of it. The element of personal choice and freedom is foremost.

MANAGEMENT
is the
universal and unavoidable
personal and organizational process
of relating
resources to objectives.

EDUCATIONAL MANAGEMENT
is the
particular process of relating
resources to objectives
required in organizations which
explicitly exist to provide education.

In contrast, 'management' and 'educational management' are inescapably concerned with *confining* freedom of action. They seek to encourage selective behaviour and a limited interpretation of events in the service of particular objectives. This is a condition of course which affects all organization members, including those who formally occupy management positions. Both the organizational members and the physical or non-human resources which they command are intentionally devoted to the realization of specific outcomes. Certain behaviour is therefore legitimate in that it manifestly contributes to the desired ends. Other behaviour is not legitimate in that it does not contribute to the desired ends or it may actually prevent the organization from reaching them, or retard its progress towards them.

Confusion may arise in schools because in the act of being 'educated' one is also being 'managed'. In addition, the corollary applies. In the act of managing in organizations, one is hopefully learning and, therefore, undergoing an educational experience.

In schools and other educational institutions, the similarity of these concepts and their interrelatedness may easily lead to confusion. The critical distinction, however, must constantly be borne in mind. Managerial behaviour is directed towards the prescribed and limited use of human and non-human resources in order to achieve collectively explicit and desired results.

Failure to understand the differences between the concepts 'education' and 'management' may cause imbalances in organizations. In organizations generally, insufficient recognition of the 'education' process that should take place among members to accommodate the ups and downs of commercial and economic life may lead to mechanical and ineffective 'management'. In schools and other educational organizations, on the other hand, the lack of clear recognition and understanding of 'management' may create an unbusinesslike attitude and climate. Time spent in meetings, for example, may be grossly squandered whilst the opportunity is afforded for members to conduct 'academic' exercises and indulge in rhetoric which may be appropriate in the seminar or classroom discussion but lacks relevance to the effective despatch of business and the taking of decisions.

In conclusion, 'education' and 'management' can and should co-exist for the health of an organization. In schools they are both very much in evidence but the respective domains of each and the critical distinction between them need to be professionally understood and reflected in practice.

School as a workplace

As a day-to-day workplace the school consists of a large number of people – teaching staff, non-teaching staff and pupils – working together variously in large or small groups or working alone.

In primary schools it is the common mode for pupils to be in classes, each with an assigned teacher who plans the entire teaching–learning programme, or certainly the greater part of it. This might be done in collaboration with other teachers to ensure coherence, progression and effective coordination throughout the school. In contrast, it might be left completely to the teacher concerned to design it alone. In both cases the class teacher supervises the programme at the stage of implementation. Any of a large range of methods, which variously involve the teacher and the pupils, may be adopted. The choice depends upon the kind of work being undertaken and the interests, capabilities and needs of the pupils as well as the skills and experience of the teacher.

Many reasons are advanced to justify class teaching. Among the most important is the child's need for a measure of social security and emotional stability. The teacher is enabled to understand the personality and interests of each child. The child is exposed to the values and standards of one teacher only, corresponding to the idea in classical organization theory that it is best for an individual to report to only one person.

In the case of team teaching, the responsibility for providing the programme devolves on two or more teachers acting conjointly with respect to a correspondingly larger group of pupils than a class. Planning, teaching and other duties are shared, and the pupils become familiar with different values and standards as they learn to work with different members of the team, rather than exclusively with a class teacher. Numerous advantages have been identified for this way of teaching (e.g.

Forward 1971). One of the most important benefits is that of enabling the pupil to get used to working in a more complex organization.

In secondary schools the dominant feature is that pupils meet many teachers in the course of a week's work. Each of these teachers offers a limited, specialized contribution to the pupil's programme. By definition, teacher and pupil are less well known to, and understood by, each other. The pupil is exposed to many different and sometimes contradictory values and standards. There is a recognition of the growing physical and emotional independence of the young person, as well as the differentiation of their abilities and occupational destinations.

Whatever the kind of school and the particular modes which are adopted by teachers and pupils for working together, it is seldom that they will work in isolation for very long. Schools may become the place of work almost daily for a succession of other people who enter the school for a variety of purposes. They may be classed as either 'official' visitors or 'unofficial' visitors.

Among official visitors to the school are Her Majesty's Inspectorate, who monitor all dimensions of the education service. They have right of entry for a wide variety of purposes, though actual visits in the case of a particular school are generally infrequent. Contacts are conducted in a cordial, informal manner and are usually free from the kind of forbidding relationships which the term 'Inspectorate' suggests (Department of Education and Science 1970). The Local Education Authority (LEA) has right of entry for regulatory purposes through its education officers and advisers, and for maintenance purposes through its staff who are responsible for architecture, building, heating, lighting and other services, the supply of educational consumer goods, furniture and equipment, and deliveries and collections in connection with the school's catering facilities. In addition, the publicly appointed governors of the school, in their role as watchdogs of the public interest, have right of free access.

A further category consists of personnel in various social services which have a legal or quasi-legal interest in the health and welfare of children. Numbered among them are the medical and dental services, psychological services, the police, the probation service and a variety of officers concerned with the care and condition of children in families. Finally, other educational institutions expect – and are normally granted – right of access. Staff from similar schools often frequent or are invited to visit a school for purposes of professional study. For example, liaison staff from infant or first schools may exchange visits with their colleagues from the junior or middle schools to which they relate. Similarly, this may happen between junior or middle schools and related secondary schools, and between the latter and related upper schools or Further Education colleges. In addition, as is commonly the case, if a school has agreed to offer opportunities for field experience to student-teachers as part of initial teacher-education programmes, it will then grant right of access to the staff of the college, polytechnic or university who are involved in tutorial and supervisory duties in respect of the student-teacher.

Unofficial visitors fall into three main categories. Foremost are the parents who wish to speak with the head or other staff or who have been invited to discuss matters concerning their children. A second category includes people who call for exceptional or intermittent purposes, such as to undertake research, to lodge complaints or to offer materials and facilities for the use of the school. The third consists of commercial representatives, visiting by invitation or on a speculative basis. Direct contact between publishers and manufacturers and schools is on a restricted scale. The sheer volume of lines is so great that LEAs have developed central buying and distribution facilities. Commercial firms and other bodies, however, may still keep schools informed of their products and services by mail and make visits to schools to give demonstrations and advice.

Pupils and teachers leave the school premises for many approved purposes during the working day. External activities of great variety have come to be regarded as an extensive and legitimate part of the curriculum for pupils of all ages, as the following statements make clear. The first example from a junior school was supplied on request by the head of school. The second is an extract from a secondary school's handbook to parents and pupils.

> *Junior school.* The early years of schooling are ones when the mind is being stimulated as children are presented with new experiences. Our intention is through activities in and out of the classroom to make their lives as full and purposeful as possible. To this end we are able to offer involvement under three headings, Extra-Curricular, Educational and Vacational.
>
> Under 'Extra-Curricular' we are talking about 'Club' activities. These take place at lunch-time or after school and may be seen as follows: Scripture Union, Recorders, Guitars, Gymnastics, Needlework, Chess, Football, Cricket, Birdwatching, Choir, Table-tennis, Athletics, Cycling Proficiency. Without exception, each member of staff participates in at least one activity and indeed in the case of Recorders and Needlework there are four teachers involved at one time.
>
> Visits under the heading of 'Educational' are arranged as part of either a course of study being undertaken or as an initial stimulus. Examples include visits to the Weald and Downland Museum at Singleton, the Kennet and Avon Canal, and Berkshire College of Agriculture at Burchett's Green. In addition, clubs have undertaken visits to Slimbridge (Birdwatchers) and the Royal Festival Hall (Music) for one of the Ernest Reed Concerts.
>
> Vacational visits include a week's visit for pupils in their final year to a different part of either England or Wales. These visits may be termed holidays by some but from our point of view we see them

as an ideal opportunity for the classroom to become alive.
Preparatory work is carried out prior to departure with follow up
sessions whilst away and on our return.

This year we will be staying in Barmouth, North Wales, and
excursions will include, for example, a visit to a slate mine, Harlech
and Conway Castles, climbing Cader Idris and pony trekking.

We are becoming more and more conscious of rising costs and the
position that parents can be put in. This factor is going to determine
the nature of educational visits in the future. (Source: Emmbrook
County Junior School, Wokingham 1980)

Secondary School. Education does not begin and end in the
classroom. We believe very firmly in broadening horizons both
metaphorically and physically. Thus excursions and visits to a
variety of venues are very much part of the school curriculum.
These visits come under three headings, Educational, Vocational and
Vacational.

Under the first heading will be included such things as visits to the
Science Museum; London art galleries; biology and ecology courses
at Whipsnade Zoo; the sewage works; the Geography Department's
regular field trips to Swanage and Margate; the English
Department's visits to theatres which are performing works being
studied; and, likewise, visits to concerts, e.g. at Kneller Hall,
arranged by the Music Department.

With the emphasis placed on careers guidance, we also plan many
visits to aid pupils in understanding industry, commerce and the
world of work in general. For example, each year groups go to the
Barclays Bank training school in Teddington and also visit many
commercial and industrial enterprises in the vicinity.

The third group of visits, while they may appear to be holidays,
are, of course, also a part of learning in a broad sense, and every year
at least one visit abroad takes place. Usually ski-ing holidays
alternate with stays in France. However, as costs for foreign trips
are quite high we also take parties to South Wales for pony trekking
and camping, the Lake District for mountaineering pursuits, and for
many years we have taken large parties to Cornwall at Easter time.
(Langley County Secondary School 1979:14)

All these activities and movements undertaken by the pupils, staff
and others as a whole may be understood and depicted as the work of the
school. The purpose of it all is to provide a programme of experiences for
young people which will have an educating effect. This complex network
of transactions and interactions is the subject of this book. It is a study of
the complete school in action – a study of the school as a total
organization. Making such a study is as feasible in the case of the school
as it is in the case of a firm in manufacturing industry or commerce, or
another public service, and is just as necessary for the purpose of
managing the organization well.

It is unfortunate that some teachers imply that it is disreputable or inapplicable to regard the school as an organization which by definition must be managed. Such views are based on the belief that specific practices used in other kinds of organization cannot or should not be adopted in teaching. They contain the assumption that behind the practices and techniques to which exception is taken, lie values and attitudes which are somehow reprehensible and inimical to teaching and the interests of children and the education process. This is usually an unexamined assumption, however, which often does an injustice to the attitudes and practices of managers in manufacturing and commerce. The main reason for it seems to lie in the belief that management is non-human and that good management implies being devoid of concern for people. At the same time this assumption may be a convenient excuse in schools for not taking the kind of action needed to achieve effective organization. Such action may involve objective criteria that may *appear* to leave people out but which in reality are intended to safeguard and improve the lot of the organization's members. One author has pointed out that the issue is focused in the argument that 'institutions themselves are the cause of individuals' discontent and frustration ... the whole idea of organisation is anathema, a denial of human values and human interaction'. (Glatter 1973:11)

It is naturally expected that heads of schools and senior teachers are able to understand the school in its totality: it is in the nature of their jobs to do so. However, assistant teachers at all levels need to be encouraged to understand the school as an organization for three reasons. First, the individual teacher's work can be more constructively and effectively discharged if the whole to which he or she is contributing a part is fully known and understood. This is particularly important since the functional specialization to which teaching staff are often accustomed – teaching the same class or the single subject – can so easily be a handicap to an understanding of the organization as a whole (Hacon 1961). Secondly, it is characteristic of professional status to have an understanding of the whole and to take an active interest in the problems of the whole as well as the part. An increasing understanding of the whole school is certainly a necessary feature of the preparation for promotion. Thirdly, many heads and senior staff involve other staff in the management work of their schools and public pressures are being exerted to increase such involvement (Department of Education and Science, 1977c).

Uses of the word 'organization'

The term organization is used in teaching with a variety of meanings. The individual teacher may speak of being 'well organized' when he feels on top of his work. This probably means that a programme of activities for every part of his teaching work has been thought through and prepared ahead of time. If this is actually achieved it relieves the teacher of the anxiety created when preparation is left to the last minute prior to implementation. If materials are made ready and a plan of action has been charted, the teacher is free to take care of contingencies, and to concentrate on assisting the pupils when the time comes to engage in the learning activity.

Similarly, teachers speak of a colleague as being well organized or disorganized, according to the degree of reliability which they find they can place on him or her. Teachers who are constantly weighed down and preoccupied with what is going to happen in their own classes are unlikely to be able to assist a colleague or share constructively in the wider activities and responsibilities which must be borne by the teaching staff of the school as a whole. A teacher may also be judged well organized in terms of how his pupils behave. Other teachers may readily perceive that the behaviour of a colleague's pupils and the level of their work are of an acceptable standard as a result of his adequate preparation and leadership.

In addition, organization is also used to refer to the way in which the tangible objects in a school and classroom are used. The term is often used with regard to the functions given to certain rooms, areas, corridors and surfaces, the location of equipment, storage facilities and resources, and the frequency, extent, quality and visual appeal of exhibitions of materials and work. A well organized classroom can mean that the furniture, fittings, equipment and materials – in short all the *physical* objects – are arranged in the best order for the work in hand. The criterion for judging this may contain considerations of safety, ease of access, speed, quietness and availability for sharing scarce items among many pupils.

These uses of the word organization in teaching stem from the use of the verb 'to organize'. Thus, the classroom's physical objects and consumable resources need to be organized in the same sense that teachers think that they must be ready to organize the pupils. Equally, teachers may think that they should organize their colleagues, from time to time and for various reasons, if agreed activities are to be successful.

Organization as people

Organization as a noun needs to have a specific and restricted meaning. Hence, a number of preliminary points may be made about the identity and nature of organization when used in relation to management. In the first place, organization is not things but people. The organization is the people who inhabit the institution. They have come together on the basis of declared interests and purposes which they find reasonably compatible. 'Organizations are grand strategies individuals create to achieve objectives that require the effort of many.' (Argyris 1960:24)

The use made of buildings, materials, equipment and money depends on human intervention. Thus the lay-out of the classroom which earns the favourable or unfavourable comments of visitors to the school is merely a physical arrangement. Behind the state of the classroom, however, lie the thought and action of the teacher and the behavioural procedures which have been inculcated in the pupils. Behind these lie the thought and action of other staff and those in senior positions in the school.

In thinking of organization in this way it is plain that organization is a pervasive human phenomenon. Everywhere people get together to tackle difficult undertakings. Throughout the world of manufacturing and commerce, welfare and security services, sport and leisure pursuits, people organize themselves to produce goods and services.

> Organization is people, not things

The question of which people in a school make up the organization, however, is a difficult one. The size of the school in part determines the size of the organizational membership, but the nature of the composition is open to different interpretations in different schools. The teaching staff are clearly accepted as the most eligible, less so the non-teaching staff. The pupils are thought of as members in some schools, but not in others. Visitors and auxiliary helpers such as parents are probably seldom regarded as members. It is never easy to draw the boundary line around the organizational membership. Even if tangible criteria are used such as 'place of work', 'source of remuneration' or 'nature of appointment', there is still the intangible or psychological criterion concerned with how people *feel* about the organization. On the latter basis, some people who have no tangible grounds for being counted as members may well be regarded as such on psychological grounds. Similarly, those who are paid members of staff, for example, may feel alienated and non-members.

Organization as inclusive behaviour

The study of a particular organization must take into account *all the behaviour* which characterizes the group of people concerned. This includes behaviour which is wanted and that which is incidental or unexpected (Kynaston Reeves 1967). Organization consists of 'networks of relationships between people acting and reacting on each other, sometimes in accordance with intended ways of furthering the purpose of the organization; sometimes in ways which are intended, though not in terms of the official purpose; and sometimes in ways not intended by anyone'. (Emmet 1967:184)

Behavioural transactions *between* people in the course of their work form the most obvious example. Less obvious is the behaviour directed towards inanimate objects, as when working with machines or on materials for productive purposes. Least obvious but of great importance is behaviour which is not transmitted to others or directed towards objects but may be interpreted by others as signs or symptoms of the individual's physical and psychological condition as a member of the organization. This may vary from behaviour which can be interpreted as evidence of contentment and absorption in the job to that which is evidence of stress and incipient breakdown.

Although organization may be said to exist, therefore, when there are people with an ability to communicate, a willingness to contribute and who have aims and purposes in common (Barnard 1964), the human behaviour of which organization consists should be seen to include both *rational* and *non-rational* elements. In the early part of this century it was sometimes assumed that the concept of organization could be confined to what was rational (Taylor 1947). People might then be too readily regarded as passive, and subject to similar laws and predictability as physical objects. Taking such a position about organization members assumes that what may be planned may be implemented, since if people fail to cooperate with that plan, ways and means can be found to produce the necessary cooperation (Etzioni 1961; 1964). At the opposite extreme, the concept of organization in recent times has been enlarged to admit the non-rational side of human conduct (Hughes 1976; Greenfield 1977), particularly so in the case of schools (Turner 1977).

Members of an organization may not share a real enthusiasm for its objectives and interests and may even go so far as to sabotage its very existence. Clearly the self-interest of members, especially in some kinds of organizations, cannot be expected to be coterminus with the interests of the organization as a whole (Goffman 1970). Equally clearly, however, it can be seen that the balance between self-interest and organizational interest must always be in favour of the latter since organization by definition is an expression of *common* interest. In practical terms in teaching, this implies finding 'a single and coherent strategy both to enhance the personal and professional resources of the teacher and at the same time increase the school's capability with respect to change'. (Light 1973:5)

From the standpoint of the interests of the organization, individuals are capable of exhibiting both rational and non-rational behaviour. They seldom confine their behaviour to one kind or the other alone. This evidently arises because in the transactions which take place between the organization and its environment, and between members of the organization itself, both matters of fact and matters of value are at stake. Facts and values respectively mean different things to different people. What one person sees as incontrovertible 'facts' another person may see as a value judgement. Furthermore, even when 'facts' are apparently self-evident, the interpretation or meaning which people place on them varies so much because of the different value-systems which individuals cherish. Thus, the view taken as to what is rational and what is non-rational is often held to be subjective. Nevertheless, it is argued that there is an inherent logic in every situation in organizational life (Howells 1972) which should carry the conviction of members. Thus, given the purposive nature of organization in the first place it seems both sensible and justifiable to take the view that 'most behaviour in organizations is intendedly rational behaviour'. (quoted by Dunsire 1979:116)

Organization contains both
rational
and
non-rational
elements

Organization as means to an end

It follows from this definition of organization as human behaviour that organization is transitory in nature. The actual number and identity of the people who make up the membership of an organization are subject to change. Any individuals who remain members for a long time are subject to change. Their powers of mind and body wax or wane as they age and as they react variously to the different internal and external circumstances which arise in the course of time in the institution concerned.

Organization is transitory in nature

The varying group of people who comprise the membership of the school as an organization is limited but never isolated. Every organization establishes relationships with other organizations for many purposes. A study of the school as an organization must focus not only on its internal aspect but also on its *external* aspect, which is the way that the organization as a whole relates to and interacts with other organizations. The latter are themselves constantly changing and so provide an inescapable, and sometimes turbulent, environment. For any school, other organizations include other schools, economic organizations, pressure groups, the Local Education Authority and many others.

Every organization relates to
many other organizations
which form a
changing and sometimes turbulent
environment
for it

A school needs and seeks a measure of stability. Excessive instability is regarded as a pathological condition to be avoided. The degree of stability which a school may achieve depends partly on internal factors and partly on the degree of instability of each of the other organizations to which it can choose – or is obliged – to relate. It is difficult if not impossible for the school to escape or even to influence the power of some of these organizations – notably those of the Local Education Authority – to affect the school. Others, however, may be avoided at will in order to safeguard or increase the school's stability; yet others may be deliberately cultivated. In the following example, a school has been subject to a degree of dislocation not of its choosing, but finds a way of redressing the balance, and in this case reducing the turbulent effects of the action of other bodies.

> ... school is not suitable to be used as a polling station, say town councillors ... the most important thing (is) to move the polling station from the school. 'The idea of closing down schools so that politicians can come in is monstrous. Let's get polling stations out of the schools'. ... The committee recommended that the council should write to the district council urging them to use Trinity Hall as the south ward polling station, and not to use schools as polling stations during term time. (*The Henley Standard* 1979d)

As a workplace the school is subject to constant adjustment. The reason for this is that the capacities of the staff who teach and organize successive generations of pupils entering the school each year vary in response to all kinds of constraints and demands levelled at the school from other bodies of one kind and another. Sometimes, however, the internal factors are greater than the external factors as causes of adjustment. This was very often true in the 1950s, the 1960s and the early 1970s when a shortage of teachers, high teacher turnover rates and burgeoning numbers of pupils in overcrowded buildings were characteristic of schools.

In more recent times, external factors such as financial constraints, parental demands and community expectations form the larger cause, in the face of falling numbers of pupils and an adequate supply of teachers. The school does not have to yield to every demand made upon it – it would be impossible to accommodate every demand, anyway, since many are mutually·contradictory. Nevertheless, it must be seen as a workplace which survives by constant adjustment to both internal and external factors. The organization is transitory in nature because of changes *of* members or changes *in* members, and because of the demands made of them or constraints imposed on them by other organizations. In the case of the latter, however, it has been shown that all kinds of organizations have various ways of moderating them (Gouldner 1955). Bureaucratic controls have been found to be frustrated in schools by teachers who used the pressures of the classroom as a counter-measure (Pellegrin 1976:359–64). Most factors which relate to 'success' as a school may be regarded as open to modification by the teaching staff rather than fixed by external constraints (Rutter *et al.* 1979). That is, the school has enough freedom of action to become effective as an organization or to fail by its own lack of initiative and ability.

The work of the head and senior staff of a school is to accommodate internal and external variables as part of the management function. The better the understanding of developments which all the teaching staff can achieve, however, the more likely it is that the school will be an effective organization. The awareness of this point was shown succinctly by a postgraduate student-teacher on evaluating the first teaching practice: '... by studying the administration of a school, one becomes aware of the complexity of the whole organization, and how highly sensitive it is to different pressures'.

It is right that a school should be sensitive to the many different pressures which make themselves felt, not least because it does not originate its own resources. The work that it does must be subject to scrutiny and definition by many interest groups, simply because the products of all legal, social and economic organizations are for the use of others and are influenced by demand. The school is not an end in itself, like a private sports club or debating society, even though many of the activities and experiences which pupils have in them may be conceived in that way. The school is not alone in this but in common with all organizations must account to its clients. Organizations, therefore, are essentially *instrumental* in nature, or, as defined tersely by Riggs (1957), 'organizations are agents'. In modern industrial societies they are agents for the control of scarce resources which are needed to produce and distribute valued goods and services. The purposes which organizations serve ebb and flow themselves and this accentuates the transitory nature of organization. Consequently, constant adaptation is necessary (Schon 1971). These purposes may be mundane and material or elevated and concerned with meaning. They are all related to human needs. 'A planned organization ... is capable of transforming the value-content of institutions into tangible assets with great economy in the consumption of society's limited resources and efficiency in the use of manpower.' (Popper 1967:70)

Organization is instrumental in nature

Organizations in general are the means by which income and status are allocated. In the case of schools this is not only true of the teaching and non-teaching staff but also of many other occupations – such as in local government, the civil service and other educational institutions and agencies – which depend upon the existence of schools for their own employment. Even more important than this is the fact that schools as organizations affect the distribution of life chances and subsequent power of the pupils who pass through them.

The school has a delicate responsibility to respond to the claims being made of it and yet to act as a moderating and reconciling force. Many interests outside the school are reaching into the organization to influence the experiences, knowledge, values and sense of direction which are being imparted to the pupils. At the same time the school as an organization is reaching out to others who have legitimate claims to exercise such influences. These transactions are characteristic of the instrumental nature of the school, illustrated in the following contrasting examples.

Infant school.   The head of an infant school invited a Romany, who was on his way to the New Forest, to tether his horse and waggon in the grounds of the school. Having parked the vehicle in the playground, he used the recreation ground for grazing his horse and became the centre of attention of 200 children. The deputy head of Coombes County Infant School in Berkshire justified the invitation as follows: 'This sort of opportunity does not knock twice. Education should be related to real-life situations. Now we will consider how gipsies live.' (*Henley Mercury* 1979)

First school.   Schools for young children often advise parents on how to help the school, revealing the staff's understanding of the school's work, as in the following example.

> Many parents ask how they can help their pre-school child. One of the most valuable things a parent can do is to insist that what they say, they mean. **Don't give way** to a child just for a quiet life – they learn how to manipulate you from a very early age, so **be firm**! This way, they know where they stand and how far they can go, and feel secure. If you can give a reason for your decision then all the better – all children have a sense of justice which must be carefully fostered.
>
> Teach them to stand on their own feet – to feed themselves, wash and dress themselves, to perform small household tasks, like laying the table etc. – all these things help to build up the child's self-confidence. They realise they can cope with situations on their own, and for that reason it is important they are never given anything too difficult or they will become frightened. Children must feel safe.
>
> Try to involve your child in conversation and discussion. Without an adequate experience of this the child cannot learn to read. So, wherever you go with your child **talk** and be ready to listen. This exchange of ideas makes for a feeling of 'Togetherness' and again makes your child feel wanted and secure.
>
> If you want to **teach your child to write,** please remember that at school we do not use capital letters, except for the beginnings of names and sentences, and we always teach the sound of the letter first, not the name. If he/she shows little interest in recognising the written symbols and does not want to draw or write, it is much better to talk about pictures and stories together and wait until he/she starts school. Reading must always be pleasurable and interesting for children.
>
> There are many ways you can help your child develop number sense before they come to school. Every-day things like laying the

table, counting stairs as you climb them, sharing sweets, helping
with the cooking or shopping etc., all make the child aware of
numbers and gives them mathematical experience.

The staff ... hope that your child will be happy whilst at this
school and we hope to see a lot of YOU during this time. (Source:
Lea County First School, Slough)

Secondary school.   The managing director of a Berkshire engineering firm
made a critical observation on the work of secondary schools. He argued
that schools could do more to encourage an interest in industrial careers.

New impetus is needed to persuade children to enter industry rather
than try and avoid it at all costs. Schools are falling down on their
responsibility.

Local heads of secondary schools were quick to refute the charge in
various ways, one of them making the following point:

My school runs work experience schemes where children get the
opportunity to learn about industry first hand. I feel that industry
does not take enough trouble to see what the schools are doing and
they are a little mistaken making sweeping generalisations.

In justifying the position of the schools, another head said:

From our point of view we would like to know what industry
wants. If the answer is production-line fodder or typists, then
industry is out of date and should up-date itself. There is a failure of
communication between schools and industry, there is a lack of
information and understanding on both sides.

However, our responsibility to our pupils and society is not one of
training people for specific jobs, ours is the responsibility of
educating them in the broadest terms.

We would like more help from industry and commerce but we
must be assured that the jobs industry offer are satisfying and
demanding and that they have a future.

I would suggest that it should be a joint venture between industry,
the press and education with industry taking the lead. Our doors are
open, our minds are open and we recognise that the future of our
pupils is in our hands. Is industry's mind open? Or are their minds
and doors closed?

The chairman of the education committee explained the policy
which was being followed over the relationship between secondary
schools in the county and industry:

Talks are going on now between industry and the education
department. We agree that it is up to schools to realise industry's
demands but it is a matter of two-way traffic. Industry must also
understand schools' problems and demands.

Schools cannot become training grounds for industry but we are very happy to see representatives visiting the schools explaining the full meaning of industry to pupils. We must develop the links between education and industry and we are trying to develop them now. (*Henley Mercury* 1979)

All schools. A young couple from Britain were arrested by the police in Greece whilst on holiday. They were accused of making love in public, thereby offending public morals, and of being guilty of behaviour described as 'disgusting and inexcusable'. The president of the court asked them:

> Is that what they teach you to do in your schools in England? To do it in the road? And is that what you will teach your own children when you have families?
> It is a disgrace for educated young people to behave in such a way. You have shocked the local people, given a bad example to young Greeks. .... (*The Sun* 1979)

Summary

The organization of a school consists of people – though their number and identity differ factually and conceptually from school to school. In practice this means the total, complex behavioural pattern which is collectively carried out by these people as organization members. Organization is variable and transitory in nature. This is partly on account of natural changes which take place in people and the freedom which people normally have to leave organizations as well as to become members of them. This is quite apart from changes which are deliberately introduced in the behaviour of organization members. An organization relates to many other organizations, which provide a changing environment for it and shape and condition its own need to adapt. Together these internal and external aspects form the province of management.

Discussion topics

1. If organization is instrumental, what is the purpose of having respectively
   (a) an infant school, (b) a junior or middle school and (c) a secondary school?
2. In what sense and in what ways is it possible to regard and work with (a) pupils and (b) parents as *members* of the school as an organization?

Practical enquiry

1. In the case of any school you know, make a full list of other organizations to which it relates. Choose a basis for classifying them and evaluate the relationships between them and the school.
2. Find out the teaching staff turnover rates (teachers leaving and being or not being replaced) for the last five years in a school you know, and discuss the findings.

2
THE WORK OF SCHOOLS AS ORGANIZATIONS

Introduction

An organization exists when two or more people deliberately share a common purpose. Without organization complex human purposes cannot be fulfilled. This is obviously true in the case of field sports or producing a domestic refrigerator or in operating a commercial aircraft. Similarly, in a school where there is a need to provide competent teaching in a wide range of areas for a large number of pupils, the cooperative activity of many people is required. The task is not an easy one and has often been underestimated, as illustrated in the following unsolicited and verbatim commentary. This was made by a person who had completed a higher degree and worked in educational administration for a local authority before entering teaching.

> When I actually spent time in two primary schools, it was brought home very forcefully to me that teaching at this level is not so simple and easy as those who lecture on degree level physics and business studies courses had assumed that it was. To ensure that children have mastered basic skills like reading, writing and arithmetic, are developing their physical and emotional skills and are becoming socialised into the community is an exceedingly complicated and demanding task.

The need for common ground

The important condition of organization lies in the existence of common purpose. This implies at least a degree of recognition of common purpose by each person involved. Insofar as that recognition is explicit and strong, the potential for the survival and prosperity of the organization is good. When such recognition is half-hearted or weak, the organization's potential for survival and prosperity is correspondingly poor.

In the case of schools the need is to balance the school's *consensual* function and its *differentiating* function. The consensual function is concerned with those activities, procedures and judgements which are involved in the transmission of values and their derived norms, making for shared experience and outlook, which have a potentially cohesive social effect. On returning from a visit to a school, a postgraduate student-teacher wrote the following comment (quoted verbatim): 'I was very struck by the community feeling within the school, and realise how closely this is related to the school's aim that children will have respect for one another, and become caring members of the community (in school, and the wider outside community).' The differentiating function is concerned with those activities, procedures and judgements which are involved in the pupil's acquisition of specific skills and knowledge which have a potentially divisive effect (Bernstein, Elvin and Peters 1966; Bernstein 1967).

Consequently, the object of concern in the school is to find sufficient common ground so that the education of the pupils may be effectively carried out. It must be remembered, however, that schools are not the sole suppliers of learning. In the process of education the school is no more than a contributor, even though it is a very important one (Rutter *et al.* 1979). Schools do not hold a monopoly of influence and decision in the matter of the pupil's life chances. The common ground which must be found to provide the school with the unity it needs as an organization, therefore, cannot be defined by the teaching staff alone. The pupils, in undertaking their study, are not passive in the process of education; and parents as well as employers have an interest in what takes place since they must accommodate it.

There are three parties to the educational contract, therefore – the pupil as 'doer', the parent and employer as 'user' and the teacher as 'provider'. Each party has a different interest and perspective, all of which must be reconciled if the organization is to act as a unity to achieve a common and recognized or accepted set of purposes.

The three parties to the educational contract are
- the pupil as 'doer'
- the parent and employer as 'user'
- the teacher as 'provider'

Among any group of pupils, their parents or potential employers and the teachers associated with a particular school, there is inevitably a wide range of different personal purposes to be served. The range can be so wide and contain so many mutually exclusive elements that some observers have been led to conclude that schools should be conceived as organized anarchies. From the point of view of those who manage the school the essential need is for processes by which enough common ground can be identified and thereafter maintained and modified. The energies of everyone in the organization need to be marshalled and effectively focused on achieving the educational outcomes that represent the task of the organization. In this sense the school is a unitary organization.

The energies of the teaching staff form the critical factor in the school as an organization; 'in the last resort only teachers can make any educational system work well'. (Department of Education and Science 1965: para 41). In theory they should be unified and directed unambiguously towards the education of the pupil. In practice energy is lost to this purpose in two ways. In the first place, some of it is diverted from the primary task to cope with internal complexities and breakdowns of organization. These include many things from form-filling to attending meetings, political adjudication and healing rifts between staff members. Taken together, they represent *organization maintenance costs*. An illustration of organization maintenance costs – perceived as being too high – is contained in the following copy of a letter by a teacher to a national newspaper. Incidentally, it also illustrates the change which has taken place in the assumptions of teachers to be able to give expression to their opinion on educational matters in public – presumably with impunity. Teachers have been subject to disciplinary action if they engaged in such public dialogue, particularly if the matter of discussion concerned the Local Education Authority's policy or the teacher's own school.

… those who teach least get paid most.

In large comprehensive schools such as the one where I teach the senior staff are given a much lighter 'teaching-load' because they have numerous administrative duties to perform. Almost all of these such as arranging examination timetables, parents' evenings, substitutions for absent staff, allocation of rooms, collating information on a vast range of topics, and, most time-consuming of all, the drawing-up of the school timetable, could be done as well, if not better, by someone employed in a purely administrative capacity.

One such person, who would need to be nothing more than an efficient administrator, could relieve senior teachers of all their non-teaching tasks, except those concerning curriculum policy, discipline and pupils' welfare. …(The *Daily Telegraph* 1979)

In the second place, the energies of the teaching staff can be diverted from their primary purpose to cope with the complaints and criticisms from outside sources, as well as events which affect the school directly but over which they have no control. These include such matters as bad publicity, community policies, strike action, legal procedures and vandalism. Taken together, they represent *organization defence costs*. Distractions for the school may arise from many sources – high-level national disputes, local initiative to stir up support for particular policies and, at institutional level, the actions of those who subject the school to too many extraneous and contradictory influences. These sources of distraction create organization defence costs. They are illustrated respectively as follows:

> Head-teachers overwhelmingly supported a resolution ... seeking to outlaw strikes that disrupt schools, and called for joint talks with the Government, unions and local authorities to protect children from industrial disputes ...
>
> 'We must work hard to restore the image of a profession committed to the idea of service. We must be resolute in our determination to protect our children from the excesses of today's industrial society ... never in State education history had schools suffered so much from extended strikes as they had over the past two years.
>
> The head's first duty had to be for the safety, welfare and education of his pupils.' (The *Daily Telegraph* 1979)
>
> ... members of the National Association of Headteachers are to alert parents as to the likely effects the draconian cuts in education expenditure recently announced in the Budget will have on the education provision for the children in the state sector of the service.
>
> Every parent should know that if cuts of this magnitude are made they will drastically lower the level of education in our schools. This appears to be a denial of the government's respected commitment to high standards in education and a threat to the educational and social development of children and young people.
>
> The National Union of Teachers asks all parents and all those who care about the children on whom our future depends to join us in a vigorous campaign against the education cuts. (*Reading Chronicle* 1979). Legislation to free the governing bodies of schools from political control is to be introduced by the Government. ... It will be part of a drive to take a wide range of institutions out of the hands of party politicians ... the Government's intention is to change the present system of political appointments to governing bodies by enabling those most directly concerned with a school – parents, teachers and local people – to have a major say in how they are run ... to give them a real say on governing bodies ... (The *Daily Telegraph* 1979)

There are increasing expectations of personal discretion and freedom of expression among both teachers and pupils or their parents. Social values and attitudes affect the terms on which organizational unity are based. They must be accommodated internally and used to achieve the educational task of the school. Such changes must not be allowed to cause organization maintenance costs to run rampant. Similarly, schools have seldom been exposed to greater scrutiny with regard to both economic costs of educational programmes and the content of those programmes. Official and unofficial bodies both formally and informally seek to influence schools. Again, such changes must be accommodated without

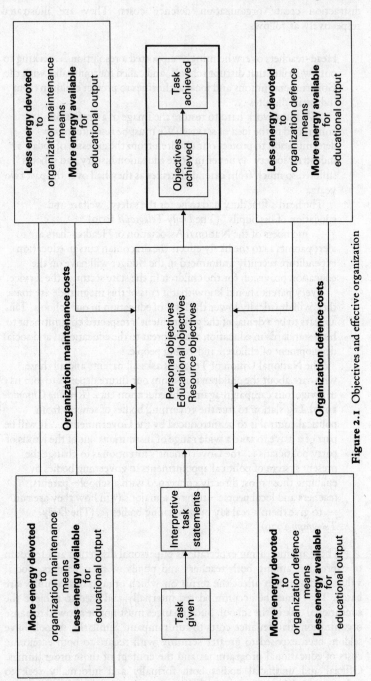

Figure 2.1 Objectives and effective organization

distracting the energies of the teaching staff by raising organization defence costs.

Those who manage the school as an organization always have a major responsibility. It is to ensure that all possible energy is devoted to the organization's primary task. This outcome can be achieved by reducing the energy loss incurred by organization maintenance and defence to the lowest levels possible. This responsibility as a factor in organizational effectiveness is illustrated in Fig. 2.1, which visually combines and interrelates the main ideas contained in this chapter.

Interpreting the task through objectives

The task of the organization may be understood in terms of the socially recognized reason for the organization's existence. The task is *given* to the organization rather than created by it, and is sanctioned in the legal, economic and fiscal policies of the community. The task given to the school is usually implied or conveyed in vague or ambiguous terms, relying heavily on convention and tacit understandings. The professional skill of the school lies in its ability to articulate this task, to make it explicit and to make it work. This involves the interpretation of the hopes and aspirations of the community so that constructive action can be taken to fulfil them.

This is readily understood in the case of the secondary school, from which many young people go direct into employment, but it is true of all schools, as elucidated in the following statement.

> ... I have become more and more aware of an increasing level of anxiety in the Primary sector – not anxiety about whether we can do it or not, in terms of holding the school in hand, or holding a class in hand, not anxiety about things getting out of control or holding a school together, but anxiety about whether we have got it right as a process, whether we are teaching what we should be teaching, and whether we are satisfying those who pay us to do a job for them – that is, the community at large. (Source: J. Killick, Senior Primary Adviser, Hampshire County Education Authority, in an address to heads of primary schools in Hampshire, 22 May 1979)

The work of the school, therefore, can only proceed effectively when the task which the community assigns to it has been interpreted sufficiently accurately and with sufficient precision. The school needs to embody its interpretation in a form which everyone understands and which provides a general guide for concrete action. The form taken is a set of *interpretive task statements*, often called aims.

Such interpretive task statements need to be formulated and given order of priority. A sample set of interpretive task statements in random order is contained in Table 2.1 and a method for assigning priority to this list is described at the end of the chapter under 'Practical enquiry'.

Table 2.1 Sample set of interpretive task statements

Learn how to be a good citizen
Learn how to respect and get along with people who think, dress and act
    differently
Learn about and try to understand the changes that take place in the world
Develop skills in reading, writing, speaking and listening
Understand and practise democratic ideas and ideals
Learn how to examine and use information
Understand and practise the skills of family living
Learn to respect and get along with people with whom we work and live
Develop skills to enter a specific field of work
Learn how to be a good manager of money, property and resources
Develop a desire for learning, now and in the future
Learn how to use leisure time
Practise and understand the ideas of health and safety
Appreciate culture and beauty in the world
Gain information needed to make job selections
Develop pride in work and a feeling of self-worth
Develop good character and self-respect
Gain a general education

(*Source:* Phi Delta Kappa, Bloomington, Indiana)

The interpretive task statements in Table 2.1 are confined to the outcomes which the school will be able to effect in the pupil. The use of a finite list such as this has the singular advantage of providing a common measure for comparing the broad priorities of the various parties to the educational contract – the pupils, the parents and employers, and the teachers. Significant differences and similarities of interest among these different parties to the educational contract have been shown to exist in actual schools when they have been asked to express their priorities in terms of the eighteen items.

Interpretive task statements need to be specific enough to relate to defined needs, rather than crude generalizations, however laudable they may appear to be. The following quotation contains examples of interpretive task statements which represent actual and emerging public priorities, with reference to secondary education:

> ... teachers generally acknowledged the need to provide more fully
> for the personal and social education of all pupils, through careers
> education and health education and by developing political and
> economic understanding and awareness of social obligations. ...
> The loss of some subjects reduced the potential range of
> opportunities, whether for employment or for continued education,
> open to those pupils at the end of their fifth year. The loss of other
> subjects removed opportunities to enlarge experience and

understanding in ways potentially valuable for the future quality of their lives as adults and citizens. (*Education* 1979:i,ii)

Interpretive task statements, however, need not be confined to the pupil. Indeed, since the task in question is the concern of the organization as a whole, it might be argued that interpretive task statements need to involve all the parties to the educational contract. The school might be conceived as a wider learning community in which change and development is not confined to pupils but must inevitably require the involvement, change and development of teachers, parents and employers. An attempt to take account of this in an actual school is shown in Table 2.2.

Table 2.2 Sample set of interpretive task statements providing for mutual involvement

---

The school aims to develop

1. In the pupils:
    (a) a background of *general knowledge* which will enable them to take their part as adult citizens in a rapidly changing society;
    (b) a *specific knowledge* in those fields which will support them in their personal, domestic and working lives;
    (c) an opportunity to develop their *interests* in the furtherance both of their careers and their leisure pursuits;
    (d) the development of a framework of *values* by which they may judge their actions in pursuing their personal fulfilment and that of others.
2. In the school:
    (a) the explicit perception and implicit application of *Christian belief* in respect and care for all in a multicultural society;
    (b) the provision of opportunities to further and share the *interests* both of staff and pupils.
3. For the community:
    (a) a *concern* for individuals and for the community in Church and State, locally, nationally and internationally;
    (b) the provision of a *succession of persons* able and willing to take their place in the service of the community;
    (c) the willing acceptance of opportunities for the school and its members to *share in caring* for the community, and for individuals within it.
4. For the staff:
    (a) *mutual respect* for the personal and intellectual integrity of each;
    (b) *support*, without intrusion, to enable each to achieve satisfaction in his personal life:
    (c) *mutual support* in the furtherance of each individual's professional life and development.

This Statement of Aims has been adopted by the Governors and the Staff.

(*Source:* Sir John Cass's Foundation and Red Coat Church of England Secondary School, London)

The need for a school to interpret the task assigned to it by the community and to formulate its interpretation in a set of clear statements which may be conveyed to everyone concerned and understood by them, is of self-evident importance. All members of the organization should be aware of these interpretations and be party to any changes which subsequently occur. They provide the ground for cooperative action and the intelligent conduct of individuals in the school. The process of underlining their importance begins for teachers during initial training, as the following extracts from reports on their teaching practice by two postgraduate student-teachers make plain. 'I had not really considered before how the aims and philosophy of the school must be clearly thought out and understood before that school can begin to function as a learning environment for children.' 'I had not really thought much about the importance of the overall aims and philosophy of a school.'

If the community conveys its wishes to the school in general and inexplicit terms, the school retains a corresponding measure of freedom of interpretation and action. This freedom at school level varies considerably from country to country. It is always open to the community to decide to be more explicit in its definition of the task. For example, in the education system of France subject areas and the hours to be spent on each are prescribed. In the English education system they are currently left to the discretion of the school.

Once the interpretative task statements are determined there remains the vital need to translate these into operational terms. Concrete action can only take place on an intelligent scale if individuals, groups of individuals, and so the organization as a whole know what to do. Knowing what to do is derived from knowing the outcomes or results intended. These outcomes or results are really changes of state which are the product of the work which is done. In a school, they are notably changes of knowledge, attitudes, skills and conduct in the pupils. To attain these changes one asks 'What is the object of the work that you are doing?' Hence, the term *objectives* is used for the achievement of desired changes of state in people or materials with which an organization is concerned.

An objective is an intention to effect a new state in oneself, other people, animals, plants or materials, revealing values, commitment and timescale.

An objective may be conveyed by means of spoken or written communication, or remain tacit and subject to inference by others.

An organizational or corporate objective is one which is agreed by two or more people who form the organization and allow their conduct respectively to be governed by it until it has been achieved.

Objectives are very often *assumed* and *implicit*, but need to be *articulated* and made *explicit*. Some Local Education Authorities are encouraging or require their schools to make their objectives explicit. This is a new trend but should occasion no surprise. The logic of it is plain and incontrovertible. The school has a task. The school is an organization. Organizations need objectives to fulfil their tasks. Some expressions of the importance of having objectives are contained in Table 2.3 (Hicks 1972:60).

Table 2.3 Importance of organizational objectives

Objectives serve as reference points for the efforts of the organization.

Objectives are necessary for coordinated effort.

For coordination, the first step is to state the objectives the organization desires to achieve.

The organization that wishes to compete effectively and grow must continually renew its objectives.

Organizational objectives are the ends toward which all organizational action is directed.

Objectives are prerequisite to determining effective policies, procedures, methods, strategies and rules.

Organizational objectives define the destination of the organization; they move forward as rapidly as they are approached or attained.

Clearly defined organizational objectives are analogous to a star which can be used for navigation by ships and airplanes.

The task of an organization receives concrete expression in the form of objectives. The *task* may be to all intents and purposes permanent – in education, for example, it might be rather vaguely 'to provide an education for children'. *Objectives*, in contrast, are precise but variable expressions of this task at any given point of time. They take into account the changing circumstances and capacity of the school as it seeks to fulfil its task. An organization needs objectives to get the best possible results, which are constantly elusive since the ability to supply 'good products' in education, as in manufacturing, is by definition never sufficient (Boulding 1953).

In simple terms, as objectives are reached new ones need to be set or existing ones reiterated if they are still appropriate. Reality, however, is more complex than this suggests. In practice, at any one point of time, many objectives are in the act of being realized, others are on the way to being realized and in the case of yet others little or nothing may have been done towards their realization. Hicks (1972) depicts these three kinds respectively as immediate objectives, attainable (i.e. probable) objectives and visionary (i.e. possible) objectives. Today's immediate objectives were yesterday's attainable objectives being formulated, and today's attainable objectives were yesterday's visionary objectives being thought about.

> Objectives define the destination of the organization; they should be
> reiterated or modified as soon as they are attained.

All objectives, and the synonyms used for this term, envisage a desirable outcome of some kind as a result of cooperative action. Objectives are desired changes of state in people or in materials which will be brought about by the action of the organization and without which they would not occur. In schools it is necessary to take into account three categories of objectives: personal objectives; educational objectives; and resource objectives.

Categories of objectives

Personal objectives
Personal objectives are those formulated by teachers or pupils or other members of the organization. Such objectives foreshadow changes which people wish to achieve in themselves, in others, in working conditions and in their terms of employment.

It is important for individuals to have personal objectives. It is important that they should be able to modify them in the interests of themselves and the community as a whole. The question of personal objectives, therefore, has an educational aspect as far as the school is concerned.

> ... the choice of objectives can be a matter of life and death, either
> for a business or an individual person. In recent times several large
> and highly regarded businesses have accidentally destroyed
> themselves by pursuing objectives beyond their capabilities, not
> realizing that they had insufficient financial or technical strength.
> On the other hand, many other businesses, by modernizing their
> objectives and making them compatible with current market
> conditions, have revitalized themselves, rising out of a state of
> weakness and decay into a new period of growth. So it has been also
> with individual men and women, some of whom have damaged
> their lives and happiness by over-rigid adherence to inappropriate
> personal objectives, whereas others have found contentment or
> perhaps new inspiration by throwing away old objectives which
> were unobtainable and taking up more realistic ones better matched
> to their abilities and circumstances. (Jackson 1975:245)

It has not always been considered appropriate to consider personal objectives in the context of organization studies and to take them into account as an aspect of management. At one time, industrial practices and social values assumed a harsher separation of the interest of the organization as a whole and those of any individual member. The contract of employment in effect was based on the exchange of selective factors. In more recent times the psychological factor has been given more recognition. This movement has had its expression in the changing general climate of interpersonal relations and differences of social distance in organizations, as a man who retired after forty-nine years' service with a national chain of stationers recorded: 'There used to be a chasm between head office, wholesale and retail. As things were you wouldn't have dared to talk to your superiors, at least not without making an appointment.' (*The Henley Standard* 1979c)

Schools, too, have been influenced by these changes, which have been based on a 'growing belief among people at large that those engaged in any enterprise, whether it is a factory, a commercial undertaking, a trade union, a political party or a college of education, should play some part in the decision-making that affects their daily lives.' (National Union of Teachers 1973:1)

The recognition that personal objectives exist does not necessarily lead to attempts to take account of them in organizations. Personal objectives are based on different values but, 'all decisions are based on values ... two individuals faced with a similar choice may make very different decisions, both of which are equally valid in terms of their own value-systems.' (Watts 1974:48)

The magnitude of the task of decision-making in schools which actually attempted to take account of personal objectives which are so inevitably as diverse, if not mutually contradictory, as they are voluminous, is self-evident. This partly explains why teachers have traditionally been expected to subordinate their own personal objectives to the common good of the school. As has been described by Watts (1976:129–30) in the case of secondary schools, and Donaldson (1970) in the case of primary schools, the common good has often been defined by the head. The wording of current documents governing the position of the head might be interpreted as recognizing the need for the head of school to define the common good to avoid anarchy: '... the headteacher shall control the conduct and curriculum, the internal organization, management and discipline of the school, the choice of equipment, books and other resources, the methods of teaching and the general arrangement of teaching groups and shall exercise supervision over the teaching and non-teaching staff.' (Inner London Education Authority 1977:11/11)

Customarily, schools have been *expected* to conduct their affairs in a certain way, being subject to the 'tendency for governors, managers and education authorities to accept, and even to encourage, the personal exercise of power by the head teacher' (National Union of Teachers 1973:1) though governors may now be advised by an education authority that, 'To the head, *in consultation with the staff*, is entrusted the day to day organization of the school and its curriculum.' (author's italics) (Inner London Education Authority, 1977:1/1).

The current widespread practice of consultation and use of participative strategies in the management of a school, therefore, may involve considerable strength of purpose as far as the head of school is concerned (Watts 1976). Given the diversity and volume of personal objectives involved, it always represents a more arduous, time-consuming and potentially risky strategy for managing (Simmons 1971). With reference to the personal objectives of *new* teachers in the school, it is not long before they discover that their responsibilities go materially beyond actual classroom teaching (Howard 1968). Teachers find that they are not free to initiate all they had intended – for purely organiz-ational reasons. They then become determined to find the means to unlock the organizational doors to reach the educational and professional goals they have chosen, or else suffer discouragement and loss of morale as part of the process of reconciling their own personal objectives with those of others.

This process may end up to the detriment of the individual and the disadvantage of the school. A teacher of first year juniors (7–8 years of age) put the matter this way: 'This is my fourth year in the school teaching the same age-group. I am not allowed to experiment with the syllabuses and am in fact simply repeating this year what I did in the three previous years. In some areas of the curriculum this may be justifiable but not in all of them. I feel frustrated and bored and this must affect my outlook and teaching.'

In the case of pupils, the fact that school makes a difference to per-sonal objectives has been re-established (Rutter *et al.* 1979) in the face of prevailing scepticism (Coleman 1966; Jencks *et al.* 1973). The fact that pupils have personal objectives at all needs no elaboration. Often they nicely coincide with what the school seeks, but may only too often be perceived as against the interests of the school, extending to the encouragement of disaffection in others or the outright obstruction of learning activities. However, it has been suggested that, 'most parents and most teachers and most children are reasonably happy with the schools that exist and they are reasonably happy with the way that the system is developing.' (Vaizey 1974)

Nevertheless, the difficulty of reconciling in the same school such diverse personal objectives as 'going to Oxbridge' and 'enjoying life' is all too clear. The head of a primary school made this point succinctly:

> On the same morning recently I saw two sets of parents. One pair was totally concerned with the academic progress of their child. The other was totally preoccupied with the social and emotional aspects of their child's experience in the school. Any suggestions I made to the one pair that there were other matters to be concerned about as well as academic performance fell on deaf ears, as did reverse suggestions in the case of the other pair.

The demand for even better organization as a way of satisfying such divergent interests has been made as follows:

If the prospect of giving a generally increased degree of private choice to all parents seems remote and if the spurious alternative in terms of grammar and secondary modern schools seems no solution to the original dilemma, the argument reverts once again to a prosaic but none the less important quest for better ways of running existing schools, better incentives for good teachers and the attempt to satisfy a higher proportion of those who might otherwise form a dissident group. (Maclure 1974)

> Personal objectives are concerned with desired changes in oneself and others, and in conditions of work and terms of employment.

Educational objectives

Educational objectives are concerned with the changes of state sought exclusively in people. They are changes of behaviour consisting of changes in knowledge, attitudes and skills. They may include those which do not affect others – for example, habits of study – and those which directly affect others, such as the tolerant treatment of the weak. Changes of state in all cases may involve unlearning as well as new learning. In the context of schools, educational objectives are concerned with changes of behaviour in the *pupil*. This usually means changes imposed or engineered but might equally be those defined by the pupil for himself.

There is no shortage of discussion at various levels of abstraction on the task which the school as an organization has or should adopt. All of the examples from prescriptive philosophy inevitably embody a decided outlook, a balanced judgement or a pronounced bias, according to taste (Nash *et al.* 1967). The school faces the forbidding problem of converting such task statements into practical steps (Ashton *et al.* 1975). Critics argue that the relationship between the declared task and organizational achievement is incongruous: 'Institutional goals continuously contradict institutional products.' (Illich 1973:111). This would be quite apparent if the task of the school was seriously to be regarded as 'inevitably to some extent a tug-of-war between the corrupting values of adult society and the efforts of teachers to help children to withstand them.' (Clegg 1974)

The *social utility* theme accounts for many prescriptions and is based on the acquisition by the pupil of cognitive, communicative, adaptive, judgemental and creative skills (O'Connor 1957). A strong emphasis on the future-orientated nature of the task appears in the assertion that everywhere there is an insistence 'on the supreme need to teach pupils how to adapt themselves to various requirements, on the need to provide them with a basic education broad enough, and a way of thinking general enough, to leave them equipped to acquire later any specialized knowledge which they may need.' (Reuchlin 1964:32)

Some prescriptions have stressed the multi-dimensional nature of the task of the school as an organization. It has been seen to consist of facilitating literacy and preparation for working life, providing a 'social adjustment' centre, acting as an agent of social change, encouraging divergent thinking for social modification, offering welfare services and job training (Koerner 1968).

The rights of the individual pupil concerned and the qualitative aspect of scholastic experiences are expanded in other prescriptions. For example, ' "education" implies the transmission of what is worth-while to those who become committed to it ... must involve knowledge and understanding and some kind of cognitive perspective, which are not inert (and) at least rules out some procedures of transmission on the grounds that they lack wittingness and voluntariness.' (Peters 1966:45)

A position for the existential aspect of the task has also been claimed. If the organization exists to provide information which is essential to the business of living and to inculcate valuable skills then it should also contribute to the spiritual development of the individual (James 1949). This has been delineated as follows. The individual on leaving the organization should:

• have acquired knowledge relevant to the solution of problems
• [be] capable of choice and self-direction
• [be] able to initiate action and be responsible for it
• learn critically and [be able to] evaluate the work of others
• [be able to] adapt to new problems
• [be able to] cooperate with others. (Sim 1970:59)

The tendency to expect too much of the school, however, has been tempered by timely reminders of the practical limits (Tyler 1967), but large demands continue to be made, as follows: 'If our educational philosophy accepts individual responsibility, not social guilt, as the final determinant of conduct, then we shall see some remarkable changes in the curriculum.' (Ardrey 1972:340)

It is tempting to cling to conventional notions of task and to avoid any attempt to reconceive the objective on grounds of being unable to meet inordinate demands. In the future, it seems that the school's task may be seen as part of a new social strategy, which involves the substantial reappraisal of the requirements of a large range of organizations. 'The normal period of schooling is insufficient to create the understanding and moral sense necessary. ... The need for a fully developed civic sense is now more urgent than at any time in history. Industry and commerce must see themselves as largely responsible for the further development of this sense beyond what can possibly be done in the schools.' (Lyons 1971:213).

It is evident from this selection of comments that different spokesmen for the community define the task of the school in various ways. These are sometimes mutually contradictory and often ambiguous, leaving plenty of scope for the school to choose its own ground. This involves choosing the prime values and order of priorities that will characterize its educational objectives.

> Educational objectives
> are concerned with changes of behaviour in the pupil
> in terms of his knowledge, attitudes and skills

Resource objectives

The word 'resources' in teaching is used in two ways. In common use it is given a narrow meaning, referring to the physical materials and equipment which the teacher needs either to make his teaching possible or to enable the pupils to do their work or both. Typically, teachers speak of 'audio-visual' resources such as cassette recorders, overhead projectors, video tape and cassette machines and film cameras, as well as a whole array of reprographic machines as their 'resources'. Such resources have transformed a great deal of teaching and learning activity in schools, giving rise to such concepts as 'resource-based learning', 'individualized teaching', 'programmed learning' and 'library resource centres'.

A management perspective in teaching, however, needs to give the word 'resources' an *inclusive* meaning. Resources are everything at the school's actual or potential disposal to enable it to reach its objectives. This meaning of the word lies behind the attempt by the Council for Educational Technology to identify 'the main factors which appear to produce successful resource organization; that is, the effective and efficient use of all available resources, whether books, film, videotape, OHP transparencies, space, money, staff or equipment, to support a curriculum designed to meet the needs of the school.' (Thornbury *et al.* 1979:11)

Resource objectives, therefore, are concerned with changes of state in the human and physical resources which are or could be available to the organization to fulfil personal and educational objectives and to discharge the task of the school. They are concerned with the current use of staff, time, space, equipment, materials and money, the quantitative and qualitative changes which might be made in them and the future uses to which they might be put. They are also concerned with internal procedures, rules and regulations, the climate of working conditions, and not least the external relations which give the school as an organization its professional and public image. Resource objectives should be highly sensitive to the ever-changing conditions of life inside and outside the school.

> Resource objectives are concerned with changes of state
> in both internal and external resources
> which may be used to realize the school's educational objectives
> and as many personal objectives as possible

The need is to marshal resources in the best combination possible to suit the interests of the particular school. This is the basis for the policy followed by the Inner London Education Authority to give schools greater discretion over the *kind* of resource they secure with the funds made available to them (Society of Education Officers 1974). Resources may be interchangeable and schools might even prefer to use, for example, greater mechanization rather than an additional member of staff.

Schools in the state sector of education by definition are subject to the direction of the Local Education Authorities over the question of the kind and volume of resources they may use. The way in which they use their resources, once allocated, is generally at the discretion of the school – the deployment of staff, the appropriation of monies, the use of space, materials and equipment, and, above all, the use of time or what is taught. Schools in the independent sector are very different in that they must first secure those basic resources before they can be deployed to fulfil the work of the school. The risks involved for a school in having such autonomy are self-evident. Nevertheless, the possibility of the inefficient use of public funds is always a concern in the state sector. It is, therefore, the need for efficiency which lies behind the argument of those who would like to see a greater measure of discretion accorded to schools in the state sector. Such a change of policy would mean giving schools enhanced powers of virement, the right to secure and manage their assets in a more individualistic and locally determined way. This would demand more advanced managerial capacity than is at present needed to manage most schools.

Nevertheless, many efforts are made by schools to increase and manage resources which are additional to those officially provided by the Local Education Authority. Schools may acquire properties which they use as holiday and study centres and loan out to other schools. Very commonly they purchase and maintain motor vehicles which become critical for the maintenance of a varied and interesting curricular programme, as is explained in the following extract from a secondary school's handbook for parents and pupils:

> The wide range of extra-mural activities is only possible because the school has its own 42-seater Bedford coach. While it might be regarded as rather elderly it is always kept in first rate mechanical order, but it does, of course, require funds as we cannot 'hire' it out. Therefore there are many fund raising activities associated with the maintenance of the coach and the support of parents is very necessary. (Langley County Secondary School 1979:14)

Small schools also undertake quite large projects to help themselves. The following is a good example of what can be done:

> ... Primary School Association made a profit of some £800 at their fete in the school grounds on Saturday.

The association, who had been hoping to raise £1,000 from the event, are to spend the money shortly on repairs and insulation work at the school swimming pool and they also plan to build a porch at the entrance of the premises and to renew the pool's water-heating boiler.

Takings amounted to over £1,150 including gate money amounting to £110 from which it was estimated that well over 1,000 people were at the event. (*Henley Mercury* 1979)

Organizational objectives for a school consist of
Personal Objectives
Educational Objectives
Resource Objectives

The critical difference between objectives

There is a critical difference between educational objectives and resource objectives. By their very nature, educational objectives are infinite in that we want the best for our children. We are reluctant to exclude any desirable outcome and therefore to assign priorities. Resources are, however, by definition limited. Resource objectives, therefore, must of necessity be finite. The assignment of priorities in the realm of educational objectives is of the utmost importance. It is difficult to establish such priorities but to do so is a central responsibility of school management. Furthermore, educational objectives must be systematically translated into a form which can be used as a precise reference for the deployment and development of resources. Table 2.4 shows a set of unusually clear statements of the skills which pupils are expected to have on leaving a primary school. The list drawn up is not in any order of priority. Nevertheless, it represents a sufficiently limited and precise set of changes in the pupil which a school may wish to achieve, and provides a very useful measure for the disposal of the organization's resources.

Table 2.4 Educational objectives for deriving resource objectives

---

1. To be able to write a short letter to a friend or relation.
2. To be able to write a simple short story.
3. To know and occasionally read from the local paper and a daily paper.
4. To be able to use a public library alone.
5. To be able to go into the nearest large town alone.
6. To be able to find the way around a large building.
7. To be able to start a conversation with an unknown adult.

8. To be able to remember people's names.
9. To know the local area, roads, villages and suburbs by name.
10. To be able to work a tape recorder, slide projector, camera, record player and to know the difference between battery and mains power.
11. To have used simple tools: saw, chisel, hammer, screwdriver.
12. To be able to write legibly in a joined hand for note-taking.
13. To be able to look up words in a dictionary and to use the index in a reference book or an atlas.
14. To know the four rules in arithmetic and what processes are meant by signs for addition, subtraction, multiplication and division.
15. To be able to multiply and divide numbers up to 100. Five times eight equals forty, forty divided by five equals eight.
16. To work unsupervised for an hour.
17. To be prepared to accept more distant and formal relationships with several teachers rather than an intimate relationship with one.
18. To be prepared to take part in more outdoor games and to use gym equipment, to change properly and to take showers.
19. To be prepared to be separated from close friends who may be put into other classes.
20. Remember to accept the complete change of status from being in the oldest group at the primary school to becoming 'a little 'un' at the secondary.

(*from* C. Jarman: 1977, 5)

The precision of objectives

It is self-evident that objectives and resources must match. In other words it is unreasonable to set objectives which lie beyond the human capacities and the physical means which the organization commands. Conversely, it would be reprehensible to set objectives that were well within the potential of the resources at the disposal of the organization. If the one is demoralizing for organization members, the other is wasteful and frustrating. Both are species of bad management since the idea of management is to get the very best out of all the resources available. The ideal is an optimum match between objectives and resources, even when conditions are antipathetic. Hence, the dictum that good management is that which obtains exceptional results with unexceptional resources in unpropitious circumstances.

All the activities of the school as an organization should relate logically and exclusively to the set of educational objectives which has been adopted. The realization of objectives which stretch resources to the full must be the central measure of organizational effectiveness and managerial competence. From this it follows that all identifiable sub-parts of the organization such as departments, upper, middle or lower school, teams, houses, year groups or classes should have their respective objectives. These should show how each part is contributing to the educational objectives of the school.

> The coordination of objectives is necessary for
> organizational effectiveness

Ultimately, the objectives defined by each teacher for a given period – an hour, a week, a term – should indicate the small steps by which the larger behavioural changes sought in the pupil may be achieved. In principle it is important to do this: in practice it is difficult to do so. ' ... complexity of organisation ... makes it more difficult for teachers to coordinate the learning of the pupils, to plan and consult together and to attain a synoptic view of the curriculum offered by the school and of their contribution within it.' (Department of Education and Science 1979:260–1)

Nevertheless, the need to do it underlies the various efforts made by schools to overcome the difficulties. Some schools make an appointment of a member of staff to coordinate the curriculum as a specialist responsibility, while some large schools may have an interlocking committee system.

If the school were completely rational as an organization, even the personal objectives of each individual member would relate logically and exclusively to its educational objectives but in practice a great deal of variation exists. In every school the personal objectives of a particular teacher or pupil will be in part or wholly eccentric, deviant and even hostile to the declared educational objectives. Whilst the ambivalence or dissent of individuals can be accommodated, the complete secession of a formally constituted part of the organization such as a team or department cannot be permitted. At least, it cannot be permitted until and unless the educational and or the resource objectives have been modified to take account of the departure which the group concerned wishes to take. An example of this would be the case of a school which had adopted a mixed ability teaching group policy throughout. Individual teachers might deviate from this principle in their classes and be tolerated.

Whole teams or departments on the other hand would have to work for and wait until the larger principle of team or departmental autonomy was established before they could practise their preferred form of pupil grouping. Their choice of practice would by then have been legitimized by the considered modifications to the school's educational and resource objectives.

The time-scale for setting objectives must inevitably reflect the work cycle of the organization concerned. Critical factors determine these times in every case. Just as in agriculture one of the factors will be the seasonal cycle so in a school the factors will include, for example, population size and mobility, the development of the local community, the teacher–supply cycle, the external examination cycle, the period of time spent by the pupil in the school, and, above all, the growth and development of pupils in relation to the learning process.

From a consideration of all such factors, a school may set its overall objectives in relation to the short, medium and long terms – respectively called immediate, attainable and visionary objectives by Hicks (1972). An example might be as follows:

> *Short-term:* viability for the current school year
> *Medium-term:* provision of progressive programme for the duration of a pupil's stay in the school
> *Long-term:* enrichment of the local community.

Within each of these overarching categories more specific objectives may be identified to give greater guidance for action in each curriculum area. For example, in the case of craft, these might be:

> *Short-term:* hire a new teacher for craft work or encourage an existing member of staff to retrain
> *Medium-term:* build an innovative craft programme into the curriculum.
> *Long-term:* provide craft facilities and instruction for adults and youth groups in the community.

Thus far, school level objectives have been matched by curriculum objectives. Finally, however, there is the all-important need for operational or teaching objectives at the stage of implementation. These are concerned with the actual activities which people will undertake as a learning experience, chosen to produce changes in knowledge, attitudes and skills. For this reason they are often called 'behavioural objectives'. In the case of the example used – craft – those involved would ultimately be exposed to a particular range of experiences in such activities as designing, sanding, sawing, joining and the like. Both qualitative and quantitative aspects would be taken into account when the objectives for each session were set (Mager 1962; Krathwohl 1965; McAshan 1970).

If more precision can be built into objectives, however, the organization's members are able to direct their activities more constructively. Success or failure is correspondingly more clear but the consequences of this for both good and ill need to be taken into account. A sample list of the kind of items which might appear in the objectives of a secondary school is as follows:

> By the end of (e.g.) the next academic year, it is intended to achieve the following objectives. These are listed under appropriate sub-headings:

> *School climate or morale*
> 50 per cent reduction in absentee rates for pupils and staff
> 50 per cent reduction in accident rates
> *Extra-mural*
> 20 per cent increase in attendance at school clubs

Establishment of two additional clubs
Curricular
Introduction of a new Humanities programme for first year pupils
Implementation of a revised Mathematics programme for third year
pupils
10 per cent increase in external examination passes.

Strategies for formulating objectives

In the constant effort needed to develop and retain as much
organizational unity as possible, the way in which objectives are
formulated and adopted is of crucial importance. This applies particularly
to educational objectives but may also apply to resource objectives.

Two general strategies are open to the school as an organization to
achieve, maintain and modify its objectives. The 'top down' strategy is
essentially *prescriptive* in nature. Objectives in this case emanate from a
single individual – characteristically the head of school – or a very small
group of senior staff. By a hard process of telling and directives or the
softer process of selling and consultations, each sub-group and finally
each individual is obliged or is persuaded to adopt them.

Quite apart from the sense of power and control which individuals
may feel when they exercise this particular strategy, there are certain
circumstances in which it is prudent to use it. In some organizations
highly complicated and even dangerous technology is in use. At certain
times organizations experience high staff turnover rates. Many
organizations are subject to direct orders from 'parent' organizations.
These cases certainly occur in commerce and manufacturing, and in all
of them it can be argued that the 'top down' strategy is not only best but
inevitable. Schools form an example of organizations which are subject to
other organizations, such as local or central government agencies. In
Britain prescriptions to schools from other organizations – in comparison
with the practice in many other countries – are still on a limited scale.
The imposition of a 'common core curriculum' or 'minimum
competency standards' by central government on schools in Britain,
however, would represent a major increase in this scale, and raise
principles of delicacy and significance which are well realized. The
Parliamentary Under Secretary for Education told head teachers that '…
emphasis was being placed on the core curriculum, or the compulsory
study of basic subjects … Even so, the government would take care to
ensure head teachers would make the final decisions as to the curriculum
offered in their individual schools.' (*Isle of Thanet Gazette* 1980)

The 'bottom up' strategy is derivative in nature. Objectives in this
case are articulated and refined by a process which begins with the
personal objectives of individual members. It continues at the levels of
persuasion and compromise when working groups within the
organization – such as teams or departments in schools – arrive at a
collective view. All such views are then synthesized and negotiated to

form a set of objectives for the organization as a whole. This strategy, therefore, formally takes account of the interests of everyone and seeks to express objectives in terms of the wishes and perceptions of the current membership of the organization.

> Objectives may be formulated by either a
> 'top down' or a 'bottom up' strategy

Just as the 'top down' strategy may please the organization's clients or owners at the risk of alienating its members, so the 'bottom up' strategy may cause the reverse. This can be illustrated in the school. Parents or the Local Education Authority may be comforted to know that certain objectives are being adopted by the school, even though staff and pupils are not in sympathy with them. Conversely, the pupils and teachers of a school may be agreed in the adoption of objectives which parents and other external agencies regard as unwelcome. In practice, therefore, whichever strategy is adopted, the management of the school becomes involved in a process of reconciliation. The extent to which this is necessary depends upon the degree of discretion which the school enjoys in securing and deploying its resources.

A teacher in a position of managerial responsibility must be able to develop attitudes and skills which are appropriate to either the 'top down' or the 'bottom up' strategy. The individual's temperament may predispose him more readily to the one rather than the other (Paisey and Paisey 1980). The differences between the two are quite pronounced as described in the following quotation which refers to the practice of implementing a 'bottom up' strategy by an individual manager.

> Far from being a man charged with the responsibility of creating policy, he finds himself obliged to feed in ideas (if he has any) at the level of departments or faculties, and then patiently to watch them from the chair at numerous committees, percolating upwards ... A large proportion of his time, and the bulk of his reserves of moral stamina, are spent in persuading committees of the virtues of unanimity, guiding ideas from one committee to the next, and concentrating ideas into forms which admit of administrative action. ... (Ashby 1966)

For a variety of reasons, the advocacy if not the practice of a 'bottom up' strategy is now in vogue. In the European Economic Community, ideas of industrial and social democracy, 'job enrichment' and participation may be viewed as part of a massive adaptation to the social demands of prolonged peace, technological innovation, less labour-intensive production and higher educational levels. Schools are expected to alert young people to changing values and behavioural norms. It seems that they may be invited to practise what they also present as precepts.

The Haby Reforms for schools in France and the Taylor Report in Britain are evidence that social expectations are moving in favour of the 'bottom up' strategy in some form (*Le Courrier* 1975; Department of Education and Science 1977a), and in the United States a study commission established by the respected educational association Phi Delta Kappa (1979) has published *Guidelines for the Effective Incorporation of Parents into the Instructional Process*.

Educational objectives should be formulated
by a 'bottom up' strategy.
Resource objectives are commonly formulated
by a 'top down' strategy
but may be formulated
by a 'bottom up' strategy

The adoption of a 'bottom up' strategy would represent a significant shift from custom if the teaching staffs of schools were systematically involved. Occasional experiments to involve, for example, the non-teaching staff as well have been tried, as at Countesthorpe College in Leicestershire (Watts 1976). The direct involvement of other parties to the education contract, as foreshadowed in the 'Taylor Report', would constitute a radical change from historic practice (Department of Education and Science 1977a).

To illustrate the kind of event that a school would formally need to encourage if it overtly adopted a 'bottom up' strategy, the following example from French education is given. It is a copy of a document circulated to relevant parents in the school district indicated, originating, of course, among parents, pupils or others outside of the school.

The teaching of Arabic to immigrant children
In the minds of many of us, Arabic is not only a language. Arabic is a means of reading and understanding the Koran and of practising our religion better. In actual fact, the whole world recognizes Arabic as a language of great culture and of a brilliant civilization.

On the other hand, Arabic countries themselves, at international level, impose Arabic as a modern language and as a working tool in big international meetings ...

For us immigrants, it's a necessity and a right to learn our language.

Do you know that your children can learn Arabic in school? They can choose Arabic as a first modern language from the first form of secondary school. So get together and make the request for it to the head of the secondary school which your child attends.

The minimum number of pupils necessary for a language class is

10. It is equally possible to group pupils from different classes or schools. At the moment in St Etienne, St Chamond and Chambon, Arabic is already taught as a modern language in certain schools.

If your children are at the primary school the circular of 1970, one of 1973, and another of April, 1975 provide for the organization of lessons in the mother language of the children ... within school hours. In practice these are parallel classes, which mean outside normal classes and therefore in addition to them, and this causes problems. These lessons are only organized at your request.

Get together, organize yourselves and make joint requests to the local education authority, the heads of schools, and parents' associations.

Since the late 1970s education has entered into a foreseeably long period of contraction after a quarter of a century of expansion. This fact has a critical bearing on the issue of what objectives should be and how they might be formulated. The social composition and ability range in most schools is heterogeneous. Finding an acceptable set of objectives in such circumstances by the 'top down' strategy is particularly difficult. The advent of falling rolls may encourage schools to cling to the 'top down' strategy. The fact that staff turnover rates have assumed nil or minimal proportions, however, is a counter argument in favour of the 'bottom up' strategy to secure the maximum interest and effort in stable conditions. The 'bottom up' strategy might be the means 'to bring together the teaching staff of a school in such a way that all their enthusiasm, all their talents, all their ideas, all their knowledge, are employed in producing a curriculum which will fulfil the purpose of the school.' (Source: J. Killick, Senior Primary Adviser, Hampshire Education Authority, in an address to heads of primary schools, 22 May 1979)

Summary

Organization exists when two or more people share a common purpose. It persists as long as the common purpose is retained. The common purpose may be viewed as the organization's task or reason for being in existence. When many people are involved as members of an organization it becomes difficult to obtain and retain such common purpose. Vague or highly generalized definitions of common purpose mask this difficulty in practice.

The main task of management is to ensure that all resources are used to the full. In particular, those who manage in schools should try to reduce the expenditure of time and energy of the members on organization maintenance and organization defence costs, in favour of the education of the pupils. Educational and resource objectives should be established and reconciled with personal objectives as far as possible to achieve results that are acceptable.

Acceptable results in themselves vary according to a number of different standpoints since schools are complex organizations in that there are several parties to the educational contract. Agreement on objectives – which implies agreement on the task of the school – is not easy to achieve. Two means for arriving at agreed objectives may be described respectively as 'top down' and 'bottom up' strategies. It is the vital job of management in the school to work towards unity, which may derive from conformity if the 'top down' strategy is used and reconciliation if the 'bottom up' strategy is employed.

Discussion topics

1. '... the broader and vaguer one's statement of objectives, the more the agreement with it ... the more specific and useful the statement, the fewer the people who will accept'. If this is true, what are the implications for arriving at objectives in the school?

2. Identify the grounds on which the parties to the educational contract – the pupils, the parents and employers and the teaching and other staff – may make legitimate claims on the objectives of the school.

Practical enquiry

In the case of a school to which you have access, collect and classify as many examples of organization maintenance costs and organization defence costs as possible. Bear in mind that the elemental resources consist of time, money, space, equipment and materials.

In small groups, discuss and assign priority ratings to the 18 items of interpretive task statements shown in Table 2.1. One way of doing this is as follows. There are 45 points to be distributed among the 18 items. Begin by giving one point to each of the 18 items which you think is worthy of consideration. Of all the items with one point, some will seem of greater importance: give these each a second point. Of all those with two points, some will seem of greater importance: give these each a third point. Of those with three points, some will seem of greater importance: give any such items a fourth point. At least *one* item which has four points should then be given a fifth point. All 45 points must be used.

3
SCHOOLS AS DISTINCTIVE ORGANIZATIONS

Introduction

If a number of people come together to form an organization, as in the case of the teaching and non-teaching staff of a school, there must be an avowed and agreed purpose. This has been depicted as organizational task – the subject of the preceding chapter. To be able to fulfil its purpose, to discharge its task, to reach its objectives an organization must have a technology. This is a word which has achieved common currency. It appears in everyday language for purposes of both public and private discussion. It punctuates reported or live debates in the mass media – whether of proceedings in parliament or of developments in particular industries.

In general the word stands for 'know-how' or the practical application of accumulated knowledge. People organized for work must follow the recognized and necessary practices which the particular work in question entails. The technology of an organization, therefore, may be regarded as the characteristic way in which an organization goes about its work. The school, for example, must know how to group the children for different purposes, the various methods of teaching which can be employed and how to design and implement curricular programmes.

Technology is very closely linked with objectives. Some organizations are predominantly concerned with 'adding value' to inanimate objects, as in manufacturing. Some are concerned with 'adding value' to people as in training or rehabilitation organizations of many kinds. Some involve few people but much material and equipment, as in highly automated oil-refining processes or in the chemical industry. Some involve many people but few materials, as in educational organizations such as schools.

In the case of a manufacturing organization it is easy to understand its technology as the sequence of physical techniques used on the materials involved. It is less easy to understand the concept of technology when used of the school, since the identity of the 'materials involved' or 'workflow' is less clear. Even so, visitors to a range of different organizations such as an engineering factory, a hypermarket, a hospital and a school would expect to find differences of knowledge and behavioural competences required to be a member of these organizations.

> Technology is the organization's collective 'know-how'
> - the practical application of accumulated knowledge
> - the characteristic way in which the organization acts upon its workflow.

The technology of the school

The singular difficulty involved in trying to conceptualize the technology of the school as an organization arises over the status of the pupil. Viewpoints vary between regarding pupils as the 'materials' which the organization works upon and regarding pupils as themselves being 'members' of the organization, with all the rights and obligations of membership implied in Chapter 2. Each viewpoint reflects distinctive values. Each implies different approaches to the organization of the school.

If the pupil is viewed as an 'object', then the work of the school may be conceived as acting on the pupil to achieve desired results. This is a matter of *operating on* nature, as a craftsman works upon a piece of raw leather to produce an object of worth, of use and of beauty. In this case the pupil could not be regarded as an organization member. The organization exists to work on the pupil. The membership of the organization would therefore be confined to the teaching and non-teaching staff, that is the adult population of the school. Imagery which regards pupils as 'objects' may be anathema to many people. Nevertheless, it helps to highlight some important considerations. Adults *know* more and must ensure that knowledge and 'know-how' is passed on to the succeeding generation. Adults have a right to expect of young people a degree of conformity and a measure of acceptance of whatever social arrangements already exist.

In contrast, the pupil may be regarded as a 'subject'. The school may then be conceived as acting with the pupil to obtain desired results. This is a matter of *cooperating with* nature, as a gardener provides the best environment he can for a particular seedling. What the seedling will become is already implicit but requires the right conditions to enable it to happen. In a sense the seedling responds only to what is best for it. When applied to the school, this imagery suggests that the pupil must have a substantial part in choosing the experiences that will facilitate his own development. In this case, therefore, the pupil could be regarded as an organization member, giving rise to the problem of reconciling the pupil's interest with the legitimate demands of the community (Morris 1961).

The extremes depicted by the imagery of raw leather and the seedling present stark alternatives. Each implies its own characteristic organization and management. In practice, however, teachers are unlikely to be exclusively oriented to the one or the other. Nevertheless, a contemporary restatement of this dilemma for the educator still poses the extremes, invites a choice and implies important consequential differences in the organization and management of the school.

There are those who take the view that it is not possible to affect the learning of individual pupils very much. The corollary of this view is that educational resources must primarily be spent on classifying pupils as soon as possible. The criteria used would explicitly reflect the predicted school performance levels anticipated for each pupil. Fixed or stable variables must of necessity be found for such a purpose. The process involved is one of 'discovering' talent rather than 'making' it. Genetic factors are recognized as being predominant over environmental ones in the creation and maintenance of individual differences. This would form the basis of a school's policy for the distribution and use of resources. Clearly, the greater the specificity and rigidity given to such a system the larger the potential number of pupils who would find their classification and status uncongenial. Negative or hostile attitudes against learning and the school as an institution may be increased. Thus, the texture of school life and the benefits to the community would be impaired.

On the other hand there are those who advocate the alternative strategy. The vicissitudes and demands of contemporary life demand that pupils in school are exposed to a different approach. The task is to discover among the variables that govern learning in the school those that are subject to alteration. The object is to control these alterable variables so that the very best learning opportunity for both individual teachers and individual pupils may be provided. This is the critical factor for the determination of the organization of the school and its management, based on a fuller understanding from research of the nature of such variables, how they may be altered, and with what effects. Among the alterable variables preferred in contrast to non-alterable variables are 'time-on-task' rather than 'available time', 'cognitive entry' rather than 'intelligence', 'formative' rather than 'summative' testing, 'teaching' rather than 'teachers', and 'home environment' rather than 'parental status'. (Bloom 1980: 382–385)

It is clear that the school is not involved in changing the state of, and adding value to, *inanimate* objects, as in a manufacturing plant. It *is* concerned with the adjustment of interpersonal relationships, with influencing or modifying individual conduct and physical and mental conditions, and with arranging interpersonal transactions. In this the school shares much in common with other people-oriented organizations in law, religion, social services and commercial services. However, if the school's concern for *systematic* and *broad based* learning is taken into the reckoning, something of the distinctive character of the school as an organization begins to appear, as indicated in the following quotations.

Junior school (7–11 years). The curriculum has traditionally been thought of mainly in terms of subject matter. It is now clear, however, that the school's influence is much wider and affects almost every aspect of a child's development. The curriculum must, therefore, include many more aspects than previously considered necessary, encompassing almost every aspect of the school's functioning. (Westwood Farm County Junior School 1976)

Middle school (9–13 years). It is our hope and ambition that we meet the needs of every individual boy and girl in all aspects of his or her development – intellectual, physical, emotional and social – in short the all-round development of the child to its full potential. (The Greneway School 1974)

Secondary school (state system: 11–18 years). Academic excellence in the very wide range of subjects is one of our goals; full effort in sport and extra-curricular activities is another, and equally important is the personal development of the pupils, so that they can work with each other, with staff and with the community. (Langley County Secondary School 1979)

Secondary school (independent system: 13–18 years). The idea of a school as a place in which to grow as well as to learn has been developed ... the broadening scope of education has stimulated a whole new range of activities. (St Edward's School 1979)

The existence of such concerns as are represented in these quotations, however, does not make the school as an organization unique. Training and educational activities in many walks of life – and not least within the frontiers of industry – may have the same concerns for personal development and accelerated learning. To the extent that similar work is being undertaken in such organizations as well as the schools and other educational institutions, the technological characteristics in all of them are similar.

Beyond these considerations finally, however, lie residual factors which *do* give the school its unique flavour as an organization. Whether regarded as organization members or not, pupils are under compulsion to attend; they are economically dependent; their age-range is confined and does not overlap with that of the teachers; there is a very wide range of maturity and ability levels within a school; the custodial powers of the teachers are great; the discretionary powers of the pupil are small; pupils lack the civic rights in schools which adults command – though assumptions about this are changing (Brodinsky 1979). Above all, pupils are being exposed to formative influences which affect their future lives as a whole and are designed to do so; they express themselves by informal collective behaviour but lack direct, formal representative mechanisms such as the unionization of organization members in adult life.

The following newspaper report contains a thought-provoking commentary on various aspects of the limited but clear uniqueness of the school as an organization as it is presently constituted.

Obeying orders from the two big classroom unions, 40 teachers at
——— near Swindon, have been refusing to see that the children
in their charge get fed or taught beyond the miniscule, five-hour
school-rules day. But it is in the nature of children to learn.

Taking the example of their elders, 13 pupils in the vulnerable
14–16 year old age group staged a protest strike.

... the headmaster, swiftly ordered them back to their classrooms.
Of course, they refused. 'If the teachers can take action, so can we',
said one of the boys ...

They were then suspended for three days. (The *Daily Telegraph* 1979)

Schools in the state system are unique as organizations in respect of
- the unselected nature of the members
- the compulsory attendance which they must observe
- the lack of collective identity which they show

Technological skills

In working with pupils in the school, teaching staff and non-teaching
staff apply a great deal of knowledge and use many skills which are
commonly needed in a variety of different organizations. In addition,
however, they need knowledge and skills which are more specific, if not
unique, to schools as organizations. The technology of the school may,
therefore, be said to have two aspects. One consists of *generic* skills, the
other of specific skills.

Generic skills may be regarded as those which are common to all
organizations because they are generated by the social values, approved
practices and a general legal and economic framework which are
common to those organizations. People are the bond which unites all
organizations within the same community. The way in which they
become prepared for and inducted into organizations, the terms and
conditions of their employment, the treatment they receive from and give
to others, and the levels of participation and job satisfaction which they
experience, are all factors or variables in common to all organizations.
Experience gained in organizations other than schools can be of interest
and use to those concerned with the management of schools. In turn,
experience gained in the management of educational organizations can be
of interest and use to those in other kinds of organizations. The stock of
knowledge of organizations at large exists for the understanding and
multifarious purposes of everyone.

Of paramount importance in every organization is the capacity for
making decisions, ranging from the trivial to the critical and far
reaching. The capability which any organization possesses for doing this
is vital to its success, to its ability to adapt to changing circumstances and

so, perhaps to its very survival. Adequate decision-making processes are a necessity for the school as they are for any other organization. Such processes require a large range of often sophisticated human skills. These include the ability to conceive appropriate and effective processes in the first place, but also skills of implementation, maintenance and adaptation of such processes. Such skills are generic in that all schools and all types of organizations must have them.

Specific skills, in contrast, may be regarded as those which are required in one kind of organization rather than in another because of the singular differences in the work being undertaken. In practice, the dividing line between generic skills and specific skills is often blurred. Not all members of organizations possess specific skills. The possession of generic skills implies the possibility of easy transfer from one kind of organization to another. For example, a school secretary could easily be employed in another kind of organization, since shorthand and typing skills are sufficiently generic in nature. On the contrary, a teacher skilled in the diagnosis of reading difficulties and the teaching of reading could not readily transfer employment except to another school. The skills in this case are specific to the school as an organization. The same teacher, however, is exercising generic skills when chairing a meeting of colleagues, leading an investigation into an organizational problem or writing a report.

Organization members must between them exhibit generic skills
- those that are common to all organizations, and specific skills
- those that are subject to special training or learning within a given organization and peculiar to it.

If technology is the organization's collective 'know-how', the practical application of accumulated knowledge, the school can appear to be deceptively simple in nature. Visitors to some organizations can be immediately impressed with the visible sophistication and complexity of the technology needed. To the lay visitor a school may convey little at first sight, but evoke greater respect over a longer period. The 'production' process is slow and the time-cycle is long. The programme which a pupil actually experiences in school is the result of a great deal of knowledge and experience put to practical use by the teaching staff. Two illustrations of this being done are contained in the following extracts from middle school documents. The first is from a document published for parents. It attempts to give the parent an overall view of the organizational and curricular experience to which the pupil is exposed during his stay of four years in the school but incidentally indicates the collective expertise which will be brought to bear on him. The second is from a private study document generated within a different middle school. If the first is the tip of the iceberg, showing in very simple terms what the technical capability of the school as an organization is, the second reveals the thinking that goes into providing implemented programmes and the exploration of possibilities for improvement.

Example 1

During the first two years much attention is paid to the basic skills of reading and writing, and to mathematics.

Several reading schemes are in use, backed up by supplementary readers, and tapes and other audio-visual material for slow learners. SRA reading skills boxes are used in all four years. Early mathematics is based on the Fletcher Course.

Groups are not streamed, although small groups may be flexibly setted for basic work. Science, history, geography and art are all developed through topic work.

We hope that French (En Avant) can be studied from the First Year, but the available staffing varies from year to year, making it sometimes necessary to begin French in the second year.

During the first two years a considerable part of each week will be spent with the same group of teachers in one set of rooms. As pupils progress through the school, they will work increasingly in subject areas. Particularly in the Fourth Year, history, geography, science, English and other subjects will be studied in separate classes in preparation for the Upper School Courses. SMP mathematics is introduced in Year three.

All children work in the practical arts block each week, where the choice of activity includes cookery, needlework, weaving, wood/ metal work, pottery, sculpture, painting and design. Music (including singing and instrumental work) is available to all children.

All children take part in physical education, games, and swimming, unless they are medically excused from these activities. (Source: Cranborne Middle School (9–13 years), Dorset, 1976)

Example 2

Some of us have felt for a long time that there is an unnatural division in the school, a dichotomy that separates the first two years from the third and fourth years. Although as teachers we are all concerned with the education and welfare of our children it sometimes appears that there are two differing philosophies operating within the school. If this is so it cannot fail to have a deleterious effect on the children we teach. The reason for the apparent division is, we believe, not differing philosophies but different methods of organisation prevailing within the school. We are all familiar with these so there is no need to enlarge on them. If we see the Middle school as a bridge between the First school and the High school then we must agree that throughout his/her middle school career the child ought to be gradually weaned away from the informal, class-based organisation of the First school and introduced to the more formal and specialist-based organisation of the High school.

One of the problems we have failed to overcome is the means of giving those teachers who so wish it the opportunity to gain teaching experience throughout the entire age range of the school, or at least, a wider range than either the 1st/2nd years or the 3rd/4th years. We do not believe that any teacher, no matter how experienced, has a god-given right to pre-empt for himself or herself teaching in a particular year group. Having said that, however, certain subjects require a specialist knowledge which some of us do not possess. Music is a subject which probably more than any other demands such specialist knowledge and ability. In addition, certain teachers may feel so opposed to a particular methodology that it would be unfair to ask them to teach in such a way. With these points in mind, we feel that this is an opportune moment to set up a working party to review the organisation of the school and possibly to recommend changes.

The first year might, for example, operate a class-based system. The five teachers would be responsible for teaching all subjects to their respective classes with the exception of Music and P.E. and probably French. This would mean that these teachers would not be asked, indeed would not be able, to teach anywhere else in the school unless called upon to substitute for an absent colleague. It would **not** mean that these teachers would be responsible for first year classes throughout the whole of their time at this school. They would be offered the opportunity to move to another year group at the end of a certain period should they so wish it.

The advantages of a class-based system for the first year would be that the children would be given a year to settle down in a new school. They would have the security of relating to one teacher only for the majority of their lessons. They would be spared the confusion and time-wasting of moving from one area to another for subjects such as Mathematics, English and Project. The teachers would be under less pressure because the children would not be moving from area to area at irregular intervals. It would be easier for the teacher to keep a check on work done and progress made and to ensure that unsatisfactory work was repeated. Year tutors would find it easier to monitor work.

The fourth year would continue to be specialist based – this is the way most High schools are organised. Also, at this level, the necessary degree of specialist knowledge in certain subjects e.g. Science, Mathematics, is not possessed by all teachers.

It seems, therefore, that it is in the organisation and methods of the 2nd and 3rd years that some changes are possible and necessary and it is to these two years that the working party will give most of its attention. (Source: Seacroft Middle School (8–12 years), Leeds, 1979)

Technology as control

The foregoing extracts illustrate that implicit in the concept of organizational technology is the need for control. The technology employed is intended to produce an organization *under* control and not one that is *out* of control.

Control is needed if objectives are to be reached

Some organizations employ means of production that are well understood and *certain* in nature and which also achieve clear and predictable results. Manufacturing organizations generally fall into this group. Others employ certain means but face *uncertain* outcomes, as in medical or military organizations. Yet others again employ uncertain means – as in commercial organizations which use advertising, surveys and impressionistic bases for decision – but may achieve certain outcomes in the sale of products. Schools, however, fall into a fourth category where both means and outcomes are uncertain in nature. The use of measures in education for any purpose is consequently difficult.

It is easier to measure 'quantity' than 'quality'. In education, however, the quality is generally thought to be of greater importance than quantity. The issue of measuring in education is explosive, since it involves the principle of formal accountability for the teaching profession, and complex, since the reliability and validity of measures are always in question. Even if they were not, there would still be an ideological question as to whether or not output measurement *should* be applied. 'Any management system which depends upon the application of resources to expressed objectives will need to develop a means of judging how successful that process has been. Assessment of achievement of the education service is extremely complex and there is as yet little general agreement on how this should be done.' (Society of Education Officers 1974:101)

The school is a difficult organization to handle, therefore, because its technology is so uncertain. Control is elusive. The ways and means which teachers use to achieve their objectives are uncertain. For example, the kind of pupil grouping adopted carries no guarantees. The properties of one kind of grouping as compared with another are not universally reliable and incontestable. The precise nature of the outcomes which are achieved in the pupil are similarly uncertain. Dealing with people who are exposed to a wide variety of learning programmes is a more uncertain business than dealing with physical objects and involves issues of far more fundamental importance. Teachers might wish sometimes that some of the uncertainty could be reduced, but are well aware that it is rooted in cherished values which actually seek to perpetuate uncertainty.

... the historical voice of genuine science, sensitive to the diversity of the human species, needs advocates willing to stand up and be counted. Civilization may have been founded on agriculture from which scientific stock-breeding of plants and animals in closely controlled conditions developed. To apply these laws to human stock-breeding is not only to depart from the conditions which validate genetics. It is to confuse origins with ends. It arrogates to the breeders a theocratic status for which their muddled thinking singularly ill-equips them. (Meredith 1974:39)

Those who seek entrance to the teaching profession are eager to know 'how to teach' and impatient to apply themselves to teaching at the earliest opportunity, but are sometimes reluctant to consider the extent of the uncertainties. This was not so in the case of a postgraduate student-teacher whose surprises and implicit recognition of uncertainty may be seen in the following extract, quoted verbatim.

As a new entrant into the world of Junior School teaching, I found it reassuring that my pre-course experience school was organised along traditional lines which I recognised, with classrooms and class teachers, rather than open-plan, and having a policy of team teaching. Now, however, I feel that as the school in which I spent the initial fortnight of the course was also organised along similar lines, it might have been better for me professionally (although perhaps more unsettling personally) if I had had an opportunity to study in depth a type of education – open plan and team teaching – with which I am not at all familiar. To some extent the school in which I spent my two weeks' study was different from the schools in which I spent my childhood as it did have a block time-table rather than 45 minutes single subject periods and it was interesting to see how the children were able to tackle this freer system; also classroom organisation, with tables in groups, rather than desks in rows was different from my own Junior School experience. The fact that children could act responsibly in the less formal atmosphere brought it home to me that the 'modern methods' of pupil planned programmes of work were educationally an improvement on the traditional idea of everybody doing the same piece of work at the same time within narrow time limits. Even so, with its closed-plan building certain teaching methods were less able to be used than I would now have liked to see.

The more sophisticated and ambitious the educational outcomes sought, the more uncertain the whole technology will be, especially until experience has produced some hard earned evidence or until pilot projects have been conducted to solve the problems involved. It takes little imagination to realize the vast range of uncertainty that hangs over both means and outcomes when teachers attempt to develop, for example, the concepts listed as follows.

For earlier development	For later development
(very roughly 5–9)	(very roughly 9–13)
Curiosity	Curiosity
Originality	Originality
Perseverance	Perseverence
Openmindedness	Openmindedness
Self-criticism	Self-criticism
Responsibility	Responsibility
Willingness to cooperate	Willingness to cooperate
Independence in thinking	Independence in thinking
Observing	Observing
Raising questions	Proposing enquiries
Exploring	Experimenting/investigating
Problem solving	Communicating verbally
Finding patterns in	Communicating non-verbally
observations	Finding patterns in observations
Communicating verbally	Critical reasoning
Communicating non-	
verbally	Applying learning
Applying learning	Concept of causality
Classifying	Concept of measurement
Concept of causality	Concept of volume
Concept of time	Concept of force
Concept of weight	Concept of energy
Concept of length	Concept of change
Concept of area	Concept of interdependence
Concept of volume	Concept of adaptation
Concept of life cycle	

(Harlen *et al.* 1977:11)

Control of the learning process

The school as an organization exists for the education of the pupil. The management of the school, by means of the chosen technology, seeks to control the *learning process* of the pupil. Conceived inclusively, this learning process has four dimensions:

CONTENT OF LEARNING
QUALITY OF LEARNING
SEQUENCE OF LEARNING
PACE OF LEARNING

Control over the learning process is ultimately obtained by affecting the pupil's self-control and by the way in which the resources of the school are deployed. A particular school's efforts in this direction will be determined by the combined operation of a number of factors. The basic values of its members will govern the organization's objectives and form of organizational communication. The knowledge which the members have of psychology will regulate the school's appreciation and understanding of individual differences. The knowledge which members have of sociology will determine its understanding of environmental influences, and their knowledge of social-psychology will determine the organization's ability to construct and manage groups. The professional background of the teaching staff — their training, experience and qualifications — modified by, and reflected in, the variable circumstances and practices peculiar to the particular school, complete the network of factors which act to produce a specific set of responses.

In practice, knowledge is used to make choices in a large number of decision areas. The following schedule has been advanced as a framework within which teachers make significant choices which control the content, quality, sequence and pace of the pupil's learning.

- Planning the nature of materials for study
- Specifying the method of studying the materials
- Deciding between self-pacing and group-pacing the materials for presentation
- Identifying the nature of the activities the learner is to engage in with respect to the materials, or the objectives
- Monitoring the learner's progress and taking corrective action
- Making explicit the role of the teacher in respect of materials and progress
- Scheduling group activities and the teaching methods to be employed
- Deciding the time limits and the allocation of plant and resources
- Assessing performance
- Providing counselling and guidance in cases where the learner is expected to share in the control as in options regarding ends or means.

(Gagné and Briggs 1979)

Models of technology

The range of choices implied in the foregoing schedule is very wide. In practice, however, certain key factors provide technology with a characteristic appearance. It all depends on the way people think about the work that they do and the way in which they go about it. In school, for example, a pupil may be thought of in isolation — as a single individual — or as a member of a group. The group may be the object of attention or it may be seen as a convenient assembly of individuals.

In studies of technology (e.g. Lockyer 1962) there are a number of concepts which bear examination for the purpose of highlighting the practices which are adopted in teaching. *Job production* is the term used when one unit of production is regarded as a complete operation, undertaken by an individual or group in its entirety. The human and non-human resources of an organization are accordingly deployed to work on one or more such units in parallel. The building of a bridge and the manufacture of a tailor-made suit are obvious examples of this principle at work. In the school, this principle would be exhibited if the content, quality, sequence and pace of learning were determined differently and specifically in the case of each individual pupil. It might also be exhibited, however, in the case of the teaching group which remained intact for all its studies throughout the required schooling period, as in Denmark and elsewhere, or for its passage through a given school, as might apply in a British junior school class.

If the work of the school is conceived as a series of set stages in a set sequence, important consequences are evoked. *Batch production* is the term used when a number of production units are moved through such a set of stages together. All the items stay in one stage until all the work for that stage has been completed in the case of every item. Only then is the batch passed on to the next stage. If all the units cannot be worked on to the same extent simultaneously at each stage, a great deal of time will be lost. Production may be discontinuous and inefficient. Items as varied as garments and motor-car panels may be manufactured by this method. In education this principle commonly appears as classes, forms or year groups. Pupils are in a stage for a year during which a teacher or group of teachers make their contribution. According to the principle it must be assumed that each pupil has reached a necessary standard in a given stage in order to be able to profit from the succeeding stage. Those who reach such a standard first are held up — as in traditional class teaching, particularly if the syllabus is prescribed — until the others also reach it. The use of the year's time span is strictly irrelevant since the principle requires only that enough time is taken to complete the work in the case of every unit. When this is achieved the whole batch then moves on.

In contrast, the essential feature of *flow production* is the achievement of continuous and progressive production in which all units are moved independently through the succession of given stages. As soon as one stage has been completed a unit moves on to the next stage irrespective of all other units involved. In the school this principle would apply in the case of individual pupils who were enabled to follow a prescribed and sequential curricular programme as far and as fast as they wished without reference to the performance of their peers. The critical difference between the operation of this principle and that of job production is that in the former the pupil follows a programmed learning path, whereas in the latter he follows an individually guided learning path.

Job Production	— each item is an end in itself until all work on it is complete
Batch Production	— each item awaits completion of work on all other items before the next stage is begun
Flow Production	— continuous and progressive work on all units moving independently through the stages of production

These *modes* of working must not be confused with the *scale* of working. Mass production is not a further mode of production but simply indicates the scale of production. A school is not obliged to adopt any particular mode of production according to its size. Mass production is critical for its effect on *quality* of production. It implies *uniform* quality rather than, as is often inferred, *low* quality.

A further set of concepts formulated by Thompson (1967) also offer the teacher a technological framework. The term *long-linked* technology has been coined for any process which consists of a series of steps which must be taken in a fixed and inescapable sequence. In schools, for example, some curricular material – as in the fields of mathematics, the natural sciences and foreign languages – are well structured in nature. Pupils need to study them in an orderly sequence. The policy for grouping pupils for these subjects should, therefore, bear this in mind. A second term is that of *mediating* technology. Many schools regard the interpersonal networks made possible by different groupings of pupils as an educational factor in themselves. Pupils can learn from each other and help each other. Examples of this principle are vertical grouping policies in primary schools and integration policies of primary and secondary education in which the physically, emotionally or mentally handicapped have at least some educational experience alongside other pupils in the same classroom. Extra-mural activities of schools, such as visits for which instructors or guides are provided and family exchange programmes with foreign schools, also exhibit this principle. A third term is that of *intensive* technology. Resources are arranged in orderly fashion and made easily accessible. They remain uncommitted, however, until a demand is expressed. When this is articulated a precise package of responses is assembled which is specific to the need expressed. This could apply to teachers as well as materials and features in progressive education programmes which are determined by the interests and needs of each pupil, primarily mediated by his choices.

Long linked technology	– a fixed and inescapable sequence of steps
Mediating technology	– arranging transactions between those with a need and those with a means to satisfy it.
Intensive technology	– resources are classified and banked, remaining uncommitted until a need is expressed.

Technology and the individual teacher

It has been argued that technology in the school is partly a matter of the collective activity of the staff as a whole and in sub-groups. This refers to the capacity to articulate possible ways of going about the work of the school, to reconcile differences and to make decisions. The fulfilment of the work of the school, however, depends finally upon the technical capacity of the individual teacher.

The concept of technology as applied knowledge or the characteristic way in which an organization acts upon its workflow is well illustrated in the case of the teacher. The following have been suggested as elements of the 'know-how' which teachers need. They are classified in two areas.

1. *The series of behavioural events which the teacher himself offers and regulates in stages*
   - Gaining attention
   - Informing the learner of the objective
   - Stimulating recall or prerequisite learning
   - Presenting the stimulus material
   - Providing learning guidance
   - Eliciting the performance
   - Providing feedback about performance correctness
   - Assessing the performance
   - Enhancing retention
   - Encouraging transfer of learning

                                              (Gagné and Briggs 1979, ch. 9)

2. *The range of media by which the learning may be induced*
   - Direct, purposeful experience
   - Contrived experience, models; mock-ups; simulation
   - Dramatized experience – plays, puppets; role-playing
   - Demonstrations
   - Study trips
   - Exhibits
   - Educational television
   - Motion pictures
   - Still pictures
   - Radio and recordings
   - Visual symbols – signs; stick figures
   - Verbal symbols

                         (Gagné and Briggs 1979:180–2: from E. A. Dale 1969)

Facing up to problems

The most important aspect of an organization's technology is the ability to solve problems. The distinctive characteristic of professional status is knowing what to think about and how to proceed when faced with unexpected or novel circumstances. Knowing how to carry on the work of the school on a directed or prescribed basis is a *technical* capacity. Knowing how to cope with the inevitably novel patterns of circumstances, in order to maintain the work of the school at a high level of excellence, is a *technological* capacity. The one requires only a *reactive* person. The other requires a *proactive* person – one who can seek out solutions by one method or another and anticipate events.

Various attempts have been made to analyse and describe all that is entailed in the behaviour of people who manage organizations successfully. In practice actual behaviour is never very tidy. Thus, all attempts to capture the spirit and many dimensions of behaviour involved in finding successful solutions to problems in the management of organizations must inevitably be inadequate in one way or another. Consequently, models based on accumulated experience are sometimes dismissed as 'mere theory'. It has been said, however, that there is nothing so practical as a good theory – if theory consists of making the past available to work for the future.

Three models are presented: they are identified respectively as the deterministic model; the probabilistic model; and the problem-solving model.

Deterministic model.   The deterministic approach relies upon objectivity, definable cause and effect and full control. The behavioural steps in this approach are as follows.

1.   Formulate the problem
2.   Identify all the variables involved
3.   List all possible solutions
4.   Hold all variables constant except one
5.   Apply the various solutions in turn
6.   Record the range of results
7.   Select the optimum result
8.   Test in pilot project
9.   Evaluate pilot project
10.   Implement and maintain.

It is evident from what has been said previously in this chapter that this approach will have limited application in the school, given the high levels of uncertainty. Nevertheless, this approach can be applied to selected classes of events. All kinds of routine events which seek established procedures may be subjected to this approach. Examples of these are the ordering, storing and distribution of consumable stock, the use of equipment, the access of parents to the school and a pupil record system. In this approach one is looking for a specific answer to a specific problem, usually restricted to objective events.

The deterministic or scientific approach is useful for understanding and finding solutions to specific and small-scale problems in schools, especially those involving routine events.

Probabilistic model.   The major events which cause concern in schools, however, are of a more diffused and non-routine nature. They are mostly problems of relationships and arriving at a suitable curricular programme for young people who are passing through the school only once. The complexities introduced by uncertainty and temporariness require a wholeness of view in which disparate elements can be united and which has a dynamic or unfolding quality about it. The deterministic or scientific approach is inappropriate for this purpose. The probabilistic or systems approach is better adapted to provide insight and understanding.

In a systems approach uncertainty is assumed. All the people, events, procedures and processes of the school at any time are regarded as a whole or single 'system'. The school is part of a larger (education) system, consisting, for example, of all schools of the same type in the locality or region – in the same way that, for example, the motorway system is part of the national transportation system of rail, air, waterway and roadway services. The school itself as a system in its own right is made up of any number of identifiable 'sub-systems' that one wishes – just as in the case of a motor-car one can identify its electrical, petrol supply, suspension, heating, engine cooling and other sub-systems. The greater the number of viable sub-systems that can be identified the better.

The sub-systems of a school will vary in kind and should be intentionally disparate in nature. They might include organizational parts such as teaching staff as a whole, non-teaching staff as a whole, year groups of pupils, a teaching team or a departmental staff. They might include programmes for remedial education or for mathematics or reading throughout the school. They might also include less tangible factors such as staff morale, pupil discipline, staff development or the school's public relations.

A systems analysis, therefore, involves an identification of the following elements (Wyant 1971).

1. The system's boundaries
2. Its sub-systems
3. Relationships between the system and its sub-systems
4. The relative importance of each sub-system
5. The order and dependencies which exist among the sub-systems
6. How systems or sub-systems may be added or subtracted
7. How a system or sub-system may be amplified
8. How a system or sub-system provides feedback
9. How systems or sub-systems interact
10. The nature of the linkages between systems or sub-systems.

Systems thinking is an aid for dealing with the complex phenomena which make up organizational life. It provides no answers in itself. It provides no prescriptive solutions. It does, however, provide a means of clarification, a means of greater understanding and a more inclusive conceptualization in the expectation that better decisions and wiser judgements may thereby be made.

The probabilistic or systems approach is useful for understanding and finding solutions to non-specific and large-scale problems in schools, especially those that involve non-routine events.

Problem-solving model. A problem-solving approach to the management of institutions in education as an attribute of professional competence is already widely accepted. Many documents of recent date have shown this in one way or another (e.g. The House of Commons 1977; Department of Education and Science 1977c).

Because of the peculiar influence which the management of a school must surely have on the pupil, the particular way in which problems are handled in school becomes in itself a model for the pupil and thereby a factor of educational significance. The possible service of a problem-solving approach in the technology of the school is at once of consequence for the pupil as well as those who manage.

The value of developing a problem-solving capacity in young people has been emphasized for a long time. As a subject of interest it has appeared in explicit or implicit form in a wide range of educational documents (e.g. Department of Education and Science 1977b; 1978). At local level an improved problem-solving capacity in school leavers is an important objective of new departures in curriculum and collaborative relations between school and industry as represented in, for example, *Guide to Links between Schools and Industry in Berkshire* (Berkshire Education Committee 1978).

The interest in problem-solving in the curriculum is not confined to Britain. Two contrasting examples of foreign interest may be given. The government of Finland is actively stressing the need to develop a problem-solving capacity in young people (Goble and Porter 1977). In the United States the National Association of Research in Science Teaching has adopted 'identifying the teaching strategies that develop problem-solving skills' as one of its three major areas of study (Berger 1978).

The question is, however, 'What is problem-solving?' Predominantly, problem-solving is a matter of method and in principle has an *a priori* and subject-free application to any activity. In this connection, it has been argued that 'what is important is not a particular fact or even a particular ordered collection of facts, but *method*. It is method rather than information which gives mastery, and it is method which must be the chief business of education.' (Burgess 1979:46)

Jackson (1975) discusses five key concepts in problem solving:
- Formulation
- Interpretation
- Courses of Action
- Decision Making
- Implementation

and, in addition, six key concepts in getting results, linked in pairs:
- Planning and Preparing
- Action and Control
- Completion and Review.

Jackson's emphasis is on simple ideas and a straightforward

approach. The following list includes most of the essential topics with which a problem-solving approach is concerned.

- What problems are and are not
- Where problems come from and how they show themselves
- How to make the best use of opportunities
- How to detect, identify and define problems
- How to increase one's understanding of a problem
- How to gather ideas and work out effective solutions
- How to choose which course of action to adopt and how to obtain commitment to it
- How to plan and control implementation so that we get the results we want
- How to assess results and learn as much as possible from experience.

Problem-solving is the art of succeeding in difficult circumstances. It depends, in the first place, on understanding the essential nature of problems and on knowing how to think about them strategically. It is important to tackle problems in an orderly manner and to acquire *disciplined habits* of thought in solving them. Getting results has more to do with controlling one's own thoughts and action than with the overcoming of difficulties. It depends primarily on being conscious of the objectives that have been established and on being determined not to waste time and effort on those objectives which are known to be unimportant or of little value.

Summary

Organizational technology has been defined as the characteristic way in which an organization goes about its work to achieve the output it wants. This concept applies to the school as much as it does to every other kind of organization. The school resembles other kinds of educational organizations in many respects and non-educational organizations in some respects. It retains, however, a number of unique features.

Owing to the complex nature of the school as an organization, an adequate conceptual approach is needed for purposes of control. Uncertainty over cause and effect in educational activity is a dominant factor affecting technology, and must be taken into account when devising strategies for solving organizational problems in schools. Recognizable practices that are characteristic of schools may nevertheless be identified and analysed, including the collective and personal skills of the teaching staff.

Control in organizations is achieved and sustained by facing up to the endless succession of problems which arise. These range from the trivial to the complex. Schools should have their own strategies and methods for solving problems. Three approaches to problems at organizational level are characterized as: the deterministic model; the probabilistic model; and the problem-solving model.

Discussion topics

1. Why is there a large measure of uncertainty in the work of the school?
2. Marshal the arguments for and against viewing the pupils in a school as the workflow.
3. To work successfully in a school, a teacher needs a wide range of personal skills. Distinguish between those that may be regarded as 'natural' to the intending teacher, those that may already exist in the individual but can be developed and those that may need to be introduced to the individual by way of training.
4. Identify the occupations to which teachers might easily transfer. Why is this so? Does a reverse movement equally apply?

Practical enquiry

Select one class teaching and one team teaching school in the primary sector. Establish the reasons for the choice of one rather than the other mode in each case. In the light of the reasons given, compare the decision-making processes adopted in the two schools

(a) for making curricular changes
(b) for appointing and deploying teaching staff.

Choose three contrasting subject departments in a secondary school to study how each regulates the content, quality, sequence and pace of learning in respect of the particular part of the curriculum for which it is responsible.

Identify a major decision that has been made in any school to which you have access. Trace the process by which it came to be made, the circumstances which demanded it and the factors which produced the particular form which the final decision took.

4
SHAPING THE ORGANIZATION

Introduction

The word structure is used in many disciplines, including biology, economics, mathematics, physics and sociology. In building and engineering fields, the concept is applied to an arrangement of materials which can bear loads in excess of its own weight. The familiar sight of steel frameworks on construction sites and bridges made of stone, timber or steel are obvious examples of this principle at work.

Similarly, when used in organizations, the concept of structure refers to an arrangement of human relationships. Given that the body of people in question – such as the teaching staff of a school – has a definable, collective task, the structure enables them to accomplish it. Structure exists primarily, therefore, as an instrumental device and not as an end in itself. It is intended to help the teaching staff of a school to achieve more than would otherwise be achieved as a sum of the independent, uncoordinated efforts of the individuals concerned. Structure is an 'enabler'.

> Structure is the deliberate
> patterning of relationships
> between organization members

Three elements of structure

The instrumental principle applies to all groups trying to act as organizations. The crew of a jumbo-jet want to achieve a safe and successful flight. The staff of a school want to achieve the acceptable education of pupils. In all such cases, the current and emerging work of the organization can at any time be analysed and apportioned to the individuals who share collective responsibility for it. The portion of the total work of the organization which comes to the individual is that individual's *job*, and constitutes his or her contribution to the organization. This is irrespective of whether or not the individual plays any part in deciding what his or her own job shall be.

The teacher's job consists of both instructional duties – working with pupils – and organizational duties – working with colleagues and other adults inside and outside the school. In both cases teachers may be subject to detailed direction over what they do and how they must do it, or they may be accorded maximum freedom of decision over both. These are theoretical extremes between which reality variously lies. In the first case – diminished direction – the job is defined by a superordinate teacher. In the latter case – maximum discretion – the assumption is made that the teacher is able to make the necessary judgements and selection of behaviour himself. In both cases the *job* of the teacher is the individual's contribution to the organizational total but the *way* in which he or she may discharge the job differs.

In attempting to discharge the job an individual expects to be able to exercise some influence on the action of others. The justification for this expectation is that each person, as an acknowledged member of the organization, has an agreed job to do in the interests of the whole. Every individual in respect of a particular job, therefore, may be said to have the right to expect other members of the organization to take due notice of the fact that an agreed contribution must be discharged. On a logical basis, this right should be appropriate to the job, and is the *authority* which an individual who undertakes the job expects to possess as a result (Urwick 1963).

Among organization members, the willingness and ability to accept and handle the authority that belongs to their respective jobs vary. Some members feel inhibited as a result of their own personality make-up, the intimidation of others, lack of training, or perhaps uncertainty. People who are new to a post experience such uncertainty. As a head has recorded: 'I had the sensation of being a stranger entering a family gathering. After two weeks this feeling has largely disappeared and I am beginning to feel part of the organization rather than a decoration on top of the cake. The latter impression was caused because I was uncertain. ...' (Quoted by Dunham 1979

Uncertainty may also arise from lack of support. The following verbatim quotation came from a team leader in a middle school.

> Only very recently has the headmaster put his full self into the
> running of the school. Until this academic year, each team leader
> was left to manage things as he or she would with no support at all
> from the top. Only if something backfired or if outside agencies were
> called in did the head notice the existence of his Team Leaders who
> were virtually running the school. This was not a happy situation.
> Things are now improving and joint decisions are made, but the
> memory of what went before still colours one's vision. (Paisey 1981:
> Appendix)

In contrast, some individuals are greedy for authority and will increase their own authority by various means at the expense of others. Difficult and sometimes bizarre situations can arise from such unchecked movements in the distribution of authority. It may happen among teachers when individuals exercise authority which is inconsistent with their responsibilities. It may also happen between teaching and non-teaching staff. A school secretary or caretaker has been known to exercise authority which reached well beyond the particular duties for which he or she was responsible, affecting decisions which influenced the educational provisions which teachers desired for the pupils.

The under- or over-exercise of authority relative to the job in classical thinking about organization has serious implications. Those who, for any reason, do not exercise the authority which their jobs require are holding back the development of the organization and reducing its efficiency and effectiveness. Means should be found to remove any obstacles to the exercise of the authority required, or to supply any assistance needed to redress the situation so that such individuals are able to discharge their jobs properly.

One of these obstacles, of course, may be that others are exerting an overbearing influence and have assumed too much authority themselves. A typical case of this occurs in junior or middle schools when the head of the school decentralizes decision making in designated areas to team leaders but the team leaders themselves do not adopt the same policy in respect of team members, or do so differentially across the different teams.

It is a responsibility of management to be vigilant over such matters and to take appropriate action. If the under- or over-exercise of authority is characteristic among senior teachers, the head of school must work to redress the situation. If it occurs among members of a sub-group, such as a year team in a junior school or a department in a secondary school, the team leader or head of department would need to take the necessary action. This is simply to elaborate the assertion that 'structuring' is an important responsibility in the management function.

In the event that a job and the authority attaching to it are projected for a period of time as constant, the individual concerned assumes, or is accorded, a *position* in the organization. A position, therefore, enshrines the expectation that a person's job is conceived in a generalized form which stresses continuity, repetition and regularity. Positions point to functions. It might be the function of a particular position in a large school – the deputy-head, for example – to deal with day-to-day crises. This he does on a basis of continuity, repetition and regularity.

The critical ingredients of structure are
job
authority
position

Job, authority and position are the elements of structure, as illustrated in Fig. 4.1. When the question is asked 'What is the structure of a school?', information is being sought by the questioner which will lead him to an understanding of the distribution of jobs, authority and positions within it. The possession of such information makes the comparison of different schools possible.

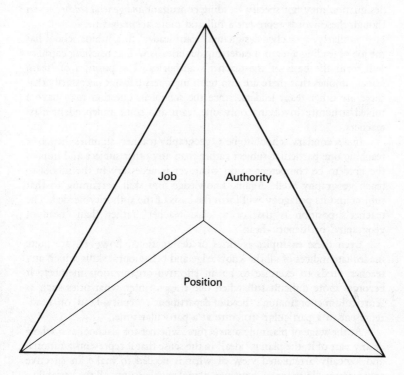

Figure 4.1 The elements of structure

The use of titles or designations

The job, authority and position of each organization member are inevitably conveyed by a title or designation, which seldom, if ever, conveys all that is entailed in behavioural terms for an individual member. This is particularly true of 'people organizations' like teaching.

It is a relatively straightforward matter to designate a teacher 'reading consultant' in a primary school to show that the teacher's preoccupation is expected to be the knowledge, abilities and concern pertinent to the process of learning to read and developing reading. The job is clear – teaching children to read and improving their reading skills. The teacher's authority will derive from the demonstrable skills and knowledge possessed and their effectiveness in terms of pupil performance levels. Other teachers will be quick to take note, unless they are perverse in attitude. The actual *position* of the teacher in the structure, however, may involve more than that conveyed by this particular phrase. The designation may not specify 'reading consultant *and general teacher*' even though these words represent a full and more accurate title.

Similarly, a teacher designated 'team leader' in a junior school has the job of leading a team. Leadership qualities as well as teaching capacity will form the basis of the teacher's authority. The position of 'team leader' implies that there are also team members but not necessarily that there are other team leaders, since the school in question may have a mixed structure involving only one team and some independent class teachers.

In a secondary school, to be a 'geography teacher' signifies the job of teaching one particular subject rather than any other subject and implies the need to be competent to do whatever is necessary in the school to teach geography well. Again, knowledge and skill pertaining to that subject and its pedagogy will form the basis of the authority needed. The teacher's position is that of a 'class teacher' rather than 'head of geography' or 'deputy-head'.

Even these examples of titles or designations, however, are quite inadequate indices of all the knowledge and behavioural skills which any teacher needs to exercise to be an effective organization member. It becomes more difficult still when one tries to infer what titles such as 'curriculum coordinator', 'head of department', 'deputy-head' or 'head' represent in a particular structure at a particular time.

At the stage of planning a structure, whether for a school as a whole or any part of it, the plan is 'ideal' in the sense that it represents a rational and logically articulated view of what is needed to make an effective organization. In practice, however, actual people – with all the variability of reality that is implied by the phrase – must give life to the planned structure and transform the drawing-board intentions and hopes into operational structure. A vital task of management is continually to match real people to the structure that an organization requires to discharge its task. In the case of the school this task is the adaptive education of young people.

Titles or designations then are inclusive terms for jobs, authority and positions. They provide a shorthand for depicting structure. They are subject to varying interpretations, according to the knowledge, understanding and expectations of the incumbent, the influence and expectations of colleagues and the intentions of those who offered the post in the first place.

Examples of organizational structures in schools are given in Tables 4.1, 4.2, 4.3 and 4.4. They are confined to the teaching staff in each case.

Table 4.1 Contrasting staff structures of two actual infant schools of similar size – 350 pupils

---

Structure 1

Head
Deputy Head
Four Scale 2 Teachers (in addition to being class teachers)
- Teacher with special responsibility for Art and Display
- Teacher with special responsibility for the Library and Language Studies
- Teacher with special responsibility for Mathematics
- Teacher with special responsibility for Physical Education

Nine Scale 1 Teachers as Class Teachers

Structure 2

Head
Deputy Head
Three Scale 2 Teachers each responsible for a teaching team (3 threes)
One Scale 2 Teacher with special responsibility for Music and a Team Member
Five Scale 1 Teachers as Team Members
Four Scale 1 Teachers as independent Class Teachers

Table 4.2 Contrasting staff structures of two actual junior schools of similar size – 520 pupils

---

Structure 1

Head
Deputy Head
Six Scale 3 Teachers
- 3 as Team Leaders in the Lower Juniors (7–9 years)
- 2 as Team Leaders in the Upper Juniors (9–11 years)
- Teacher as coordinator for Language Studies

Four Scale 2 Teachers
- Teacher in charge of Art, Craft and Display
- Teacher in charge of Music
- Teacher in charge of Physical Education and Games
- Teacher to take care of the special needs of pupils

Nine Scale 1 Teachers as Team Members

Structure 2

Head
Deputy Head, Programme Coordinator for the Upper School (9–11 years)
One Scale 3 Teacher, Programme Coordinator for the Lower School (7–9 years)
Three Scale 3 Teachers (in addition to being class teachers)
- Teacher with special responsibility for English Studies
- Teacher with special responsibility for Mathematics
- Teacher with special responsibility for Science

Eight Scale 2 Teachers (in addition to being class teachers)
- Teacher with special responsibility for clubs and extra-mural activities

- Teacher with special responsibility for immigrant pupils
- Teacher with special responsibility for Girls' Games
- Teacher with special responsibility for the Library
- Teacher with special responsibility for Music
- Teacher with special responsibility for Physical Education
- Teacher with special responsibility for Remedial Education
- Teacher with special responsibility for staff support and student teachers in the school

Seven Scale 1 Teachers as Class Teachers

Table 4.3 Staff structure of an actual secondary school of 1,300 pupils

---

Head
Deputy Head responsible for Academic Affairs
Deputy Head responsible for Pastoral Affairs
Senior Mistress responsible for Examinations and Head of Upper School
Six Scale 4 Teachers

- Head of Lower School
- Head of Middle School
- Head of English
- Head of Mathematics
- Head of Modern Languages
- Head of Science and special responsibility for Biology

Sixteen Scale 3 Teachers

- Assistant Head of Lower School
- Assistant Head of Middle School
- Head of Art
- Head of Boys' Craft
- Head of Business Studies
- Head of Chemistry
- Head of Creative Studies
- Head of Geography
- Head of History and Assistant Head of Upper School
- Head of Home Economics
- Head of Music
- Head of Physical Education
- Head of Physics
- Assistant Head of English
- Assistant Head of Mathematics
- Assistant Head of Modern Languages

Seventeen Scale 2 Teachers

- Teacher in charge of Archives in the History Department
- Assistant Head of Art
- Head of Careers
- Teacher in charge of Computer Studies
- Teacher in charge of Drama
- Teacher in charge of Certificate in Secondary Education courses in Modern Languages

- Teacher in charge of Geology
- Teacher in charge of Lower School Science
- Teacher in charge of Needlework
- Teacher in charge of Boys' Physical Education
- Head of Religious Studies
- Head of Remedial Education
- Head of Resources
- Teacher in charge of Secretarial Studies
- Teacher in charge of Statistics
- Teacher in charge of Upper School English
- Teacher in charge of Woodwork

Scale 1 Teachers

Table 4.4 Suggested contrasting alternative structures for a secondary school of 1,300 pupils (Department of Education and Science 1977b: 75 and 80)

Structure 1

Head
Deputy Head (pupils)
Deputy Head (staff)
Senior Master/Mistress (external)
Nine Scale 4 Teachers
- Head of Lower School
- Head of Middle School
- Head of Upper School
- Head of Language Department
- Head of Mathematical and Scientific Activities
- Head of Creative and Recreative Studies
- Head of Cognitive Activities, Examinations and Assessment
- Senior Teacher as Head of Careers and Educational Guidance
- Senior Teacher as Head of Resources and Finance

Seventeen Scale 3 Teachers
- 16 Heads of Subjects
- 1 Teacher Librarian

Twenty one Scale 2 Teachers
- 6 Heads of Years 1–6
- 15 Assistant Heads of Subjects and/or other special responsibilities

Scale 1 Teachers

Structure 2

Head
Deputy Head (pupils)
Deputy Head (staff)
Senior Master/Mistress (resources and finance)
Seventeen Scale 4 Teachers (any 4 to be designated Senior Teacher)
Heads of curricular contribution to pupil development
- Aesthetic/creative
- Ethical

- Linguistic
- Mathematical
- Physical
- Scientific
- Social and Political
- Spiritual

Heads of administrative contribution to pupil development
- 5 Heads of Years 1–5
- Head of Careers and Course Coordination
- Head of Resource-based Learning and Library
- Teacher in charge of timetable
- Teacher in charge of examinations and assessment, internal and external, and Head of Year 6

17–32 Teachers in support posts, mostly Scale 2 but some Scale 3, shared in proportion 2:1 for curricular contribution
Scale 1 Teachers

The political aspect of structure

With a high staff turnover, structural changes may be readily made. Staff who remain can be offered jobs, authority and positions vacated by those who have left. Alternatively, structure may be thought out afresh so that remaining staff are offered new jobs, authority and positions, leaving the residual vacancies to be filled by newcomers.

Structural changes are nearly always exhilarating for some and threatening for others. The risks involved, therefore, must be calculated. In times of stable staffing or low staff turnover, it is very tempting to allow structure to become static. It takes time, effort and, perhaps, stress and strain to achieve smooth working relations – to establish an effective operational structure – as a teaching staff. If the number of pupils in a school is contracting, it is almost certain that restructuring will be unavoidable.

Minimal structural change may well suit the teaching staff of a school. The critical determinant of structural change, however, should be the changing nature of the perceived organizational task. It is unlikely that the pattern of knowledge, expertise and experience represented by a particular structure will for long avoid a mismatch with the more volatile interests and needs of successive entries of pupils in a world where inexorable change is the dominant reality (Schon 1971).

It is not that structure *ought* to be subject to constant modification *per se*, but that structure is the vehicle for getting the work of organizations done, and is essentially temporary or *ad hoc* in nature. Unfortunately, however, the constant change of structure is almost certain to generate frustration, anger and perhaps unhappiness, and even breakdown, in some members. Teachers are no exception to the rule that nobody likes excessive uncertainty and discontinuity.

Everyone likes time to master a job and to feel that he or she is making a real and visible contribution to the organization. Structural changes, therefore, imply the exercise of political art, involving delicate and painstaking work on the part of those whose responsibility it is to initiate them. The successful negotiation and implementation of such changes are at the heart of good management. As a human process, changing the structure requires sensitivity and concern. As a political process it requires persuasiveness and firmness. Both require the ability to grasp the critical factors and the skills to articulate them. In short, consideration and initiation go together (Halpin 1966; 1967).

The purpose of structure

Ideally, the structure of a school should closely reflect the current overall task which the school faces. In practice, however, the structure of any organization nearly always contains maladaptive features. These are jobs, authority and positions which once made good sense but no longer meet the needs of the organization in terms of the new tasks being required of it. This constant change in the quantitative aspects of the school's task is inevitable. The reasons are plain: the increase in knowledge, staff and pupil turnover, the demands which parents and employers make of the curriculum, pedagogical factors and many other variables all combine to present any school with the need for continual adaptation.

Unusually, a teacher may join others to open a new school, and thus to structure its organization for the first time. Typically, a teacher joins an on-going school and will be required to fit into a predetermined structure. If the structuring has been skilfully accomplished, the school stands the best chance of experiencing smooth operating conditions. If the structuring has been careless, then operating conditions are likely to be difficult.

People are sometimes understandably reluctant to change successful and well-established structures. This applies particularly to schools where the staff turnover is at a low rate. This follows since, by definition, the overall, complex pattern of interpersonal relations implied by the concept of structure has been established, learned and accepted as a *modus vivendi*, with few newcomers to upset it.

Should an old structure prove inadequate in practice, a modification of it will emerge, based on the unanticipated realities of the personal capacities of the people concerned. In such a case, individuals lose either jobs, authority or positions as new pressures on the organization and new members within it make their presence felt.

Of the three elements, job, authority and position, the last is the one which occasions most difficulty in designing and modifying the structure of a school. Positions are signalled by the appellation of titles and attract differential monetary rewards. Positions, rather than jobs or authority, are least subject to change. Positions, in addition, are a powerful determinant of the expectations of the incumbents and those around them with regard to the personal capacities of position-holders. The idea of

positions gives stability to the structure. It may also infuse rigidity into
the structure, in that positions are more permanent and reflect the people
in them. Rigid structures are, by definition, maladaptive to necessary
changes in the curriculum and organization of the school. The practice of
making positions permanent, therefore, results in diminished structural
adaptability.

Figure 4.2 illustrates the fact that position, having relative
permanence, gives stability to structure, whilst jobs and authority may be
relatively flexible and subject to dispute. The diagram represents
organizational structure in the case of four people. Each has a formal
position, P, which basically distinguishes them as organization members.
Their respective jobs and authority, however, are subject to change or
redistribution, given the total task which they must collectively
discharge. This is represented in the central area of the diagram with
dotted boundary lines.

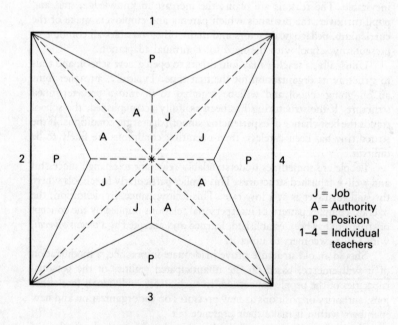

J = Job
A = Authority
P = Position
1–4 = Individual
        teachers

Figure 4.2 Structural stability and adaptation

Depicting structure – traditional forms

Attempts to depict the organizational structure of the school as a whole traditionally take the form of pyramidal shapes, either flat or tall, as in Fig. 4.3. A flat pyramid implies a less finely determined distribution of jobs (i.e. less specialization), few levels of authority and more individuals occupying similar positions as compared with a tall pyramid. In contrast, the tall pyramid represents a more finely determined distribution of jobs, many levels of authority and fewer individuals occupying similar positions. The former is said to have a short, and the latter a long, chain-of-command.

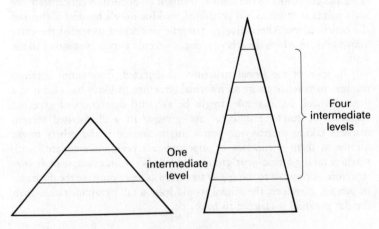

Figure 4.3 Flat and tall pyramidal forms

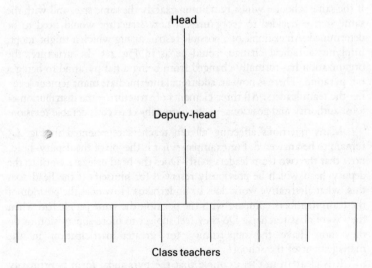

Figure 4.4 Flat pyramid in a junior school

Examples of the flat pyramid are common in schools, especially in the primary sector. A junior school, for instance, might be depicted as in Fig. 4.4. In this case, it is implied that each of the eight class teachers formally possesses equal authority attaching to equal jobs and the same structural position. In reality, however, fine distinctions are probably made between the jobs, producing differential authority, even though positions in the structure remain formally equal. In practice, of the eight class teachers shown, several would receive additional salary allowances, known as scale points, for undertaking special responsibilities. The number receiving such allowances would depend upon the decision of the head and governors of the school. It might be decided to concentrate the scale points as much as it is permitted, making only a handful of the staff the beneficiaries. Alternatively, it might be decided to spread the extra allowances, to which the school is due, as evenly as possible among all the staff.

In spite of the *formal* structure, as depicted, distinctions between teachers in practice create an informal structure. A likely basis for it in a junior school, for example, might be assumed differences of expertise required for teaching different age-groups. In a class-based school, teachers taking fourth-year pupils might assume — and others might ascribe to them — superior or superordinate positions compared with teachers taking a first-year group. This would be an example of *de facto* structure in contrast to the *de jure* structure as represented in the diagram. In *practice*, therefore, the school would have a tall pyramid, rather than the flat pyramid it claimed to have.

Restructuring

If the same school — whilst remaining exactly the same size, and with the same staff — decided to reorganize, a new structure would need to be determined. An example of a possible restructuring which it might adopt, implying a radical change, could be as in Fig. 4.5. In structure, the organization has formally changed from being a flat pyramid to being a tall pyramid. There is now an additional intermediate management level, i.e. the team leaders. All three elements of structure — the distribution of jobs, authority and positions — have been subject to considerable revision.

Many questions affecting all ten teachers represented in Fig. 4.5 remain to be answered. For example, what is the job of the deputy-head, now that the two team leaders exist? Does the head delegate work to the deputy-head which he previously reserved for himself? If the head does this, what alternative work does he undertake? How does the position of the team members compare with the position the same people had when they were class teachers? Do they feel subject to more supervision or do they now have the opportunity for greater participation in the management of the school?

It is clear from this example that the pyramidal form is primarily concerned to show the command aspect of structural positions, and

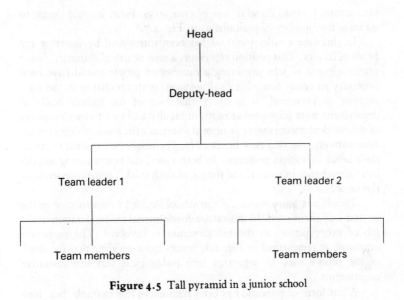

Figure 4.5 Tall pyramid in a junior school

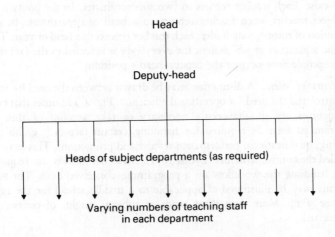

Figure 4.6 Flat pyramid in a secondary school

authority. In other words, the pyramid reveals the basic relations between people thought to be needed to give the organization a unitary direction. It shows one person as a position holder to whom another person in a subordinate position is formally answerable.

In large schools, particularly in the secondary sector, a flat pyramid would contain as many levels as the tall pyramid presented above for the junior school, as illustrated in Fig. 4.6. If such a school decided to restructure, it could do so in one of two ways. First, it could decide to increase the number of positions as in Fig. 4.7.

In this case a taller pyramid has been introduced by inserting the heads of faculty. This position represents a new centre of authority. Some rearrangement of jobs involving a number of people would have been necessary to create this additional position, with no change in the total number of personnel. It is likely that two of the former heads of department were promoted as heads of faculty and two former members of subject departments were promoted to replace the heads of department. Alternatively, the two new heads of faculty might be expected to retain their heads of subject positions. In both cases, the restructuring implies little disturbance in general and the job of each teacher remains essentially the same.

This is not so, however, if the school decided to restructure in the second way mentioned. In this case, a fundamental reconsideration of the job of every person in the old structure is involved. The particular outcome, as represented in Fig. 4.8, results from deciding that the work of the school may be separated into pedagogical and administrative constituents.

A flat form of pyramid has been retained in this example, but there are really two such pyramids rather than one. Two structures formally co-exist. Each teacher reports to two superordinates. In the position of subject teacher, each teacher reports to a head of department. In the position of tutor-group leader, each teacher reports to a head of year. The basic separation of job content for everybody is reflected in the fact that two people now occupy the deputy-head's position.

Alternative bases.   A distinction may be drawn between the need for staff control and the need for operational efficiency. Fig. 4.9 assumes that two structures are simultaneously necessary to take account of this. A pyramidal form is required for handling certain factors (e.g. hiring, firing, qualifications, performance review and promotion). This may be called the control structure (Lyons 1971). An *ad hoc* form is also required for handling the workflow on a programme-conceived basis. The two forms may be illustrated as applicable to a middle school for the age-range 9–13. More than three heads of subjects might, of course, be preferred.

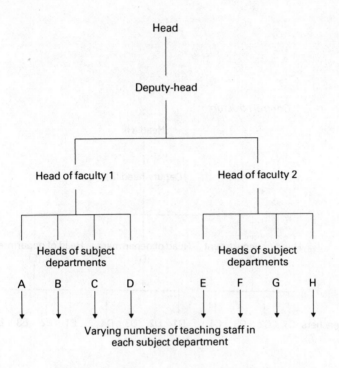

Figure 4.7 Tall pyramid in a secondary school

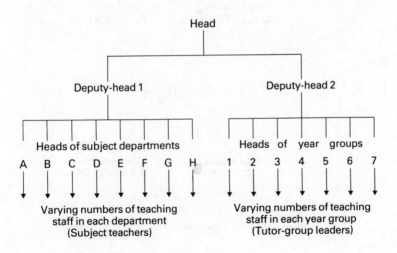

Figure 4.8 Dual pyramids in a secondary school

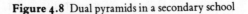

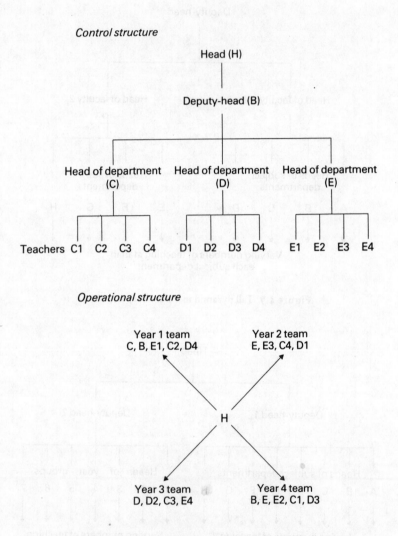

Figure 4.9 Control and operational forms of structure

Restructuring effects

Bearing in mind that structure involves jobs, authority and positions, it is self-evident that the implications of choosing one structure rather than another, and then of changing the structure, are far-reaching. The implications for the work of the organization – the educational experience offered to the pupils – are potentially substantial. In addition, but related to the educational outcome, structure affects the morale, efficiency and effectiveness of the teachers themselves. Rapid or ill-handled changes in structure can have damaging repercussions.

These factors have become important matters of concern in various branches of research in organizational and managerial studies. Many studies have demonstrated that different structures reflect different value systems (Blau and Schoenherr 1971). In the case of the school, different structures contain and reflect different assumptions about both pupils and teachers (Jennings 1975; Packwood 1977; Turner 1977). For example, it is possible at one extreme to be pessimistic about people at work, assuming that they need to be watched, directed and constantly stimulated as they seek to avoid effort and responsibility. In contrast, at the other extreme, it is possible to be optimistic about people at work, believing that the right conditions – particularly structure – will release creativity, effort and self-direction (McGregor 1960; 1967). In particular, as far as teachers are concerned, it is possible to assume either attenuated professionalism or extended professionalism (Hughes 1975).

An upsurge of studies in the field of organizational stress has also highlighted the differential outcomes from different structures in recent years (Wright 1975; Coleman 1976; Cooper and Marshall 1978; Melhuish 1978). The predicament of the individual within the structure has been a major theme of distinguished scholars for several decades (Argyris 1960). This work has been given new impetus by a focus on physiological, psychological and medical aspects of organizational structure. Within teaching, attention has been firmly drawn to the potential which the structure may have for damaging personal and professional life (National Association of Schoolmasters/Union of Women Teachers 1976).

In manufacturing and commercial organizations, the fact that stress may be caused by excessive noise or danger, for example, can be readily appreciated by everyone. It is less obvious that stress may result from the structural features and conditions which govern the organizational life of the individual.

In schools it has now been found, admitted and made plain that organizational stress is a risk factor in the occupational career of the teacher. Recent studies have emphasized the shortcomings of the school as a workplace (Dreeben 1973) and the intrinsic fatigue of teaching as an occupation (Pellegrin 1976). The most forceful and provocative illumination of this risk, however, has come from studies in Britain which attribute a great deal of stress to causes labelled as 'reorganization', 'role conflict' and 'role ambiguity' as well as poor working conditions. Teachers have administrative, pastoral and teaching work to do, but often suffer from uncertainty about the particular work they think they ought to be performing. Singular causation of stress is attributed to communication difficulties, barriers between teachers with different seniority and the kind of climate the head and senior staff generate (Thomas 1980).

When a teacher is caught in structural arrangements which are inimical to his welfare and development, extraordinary conduct may be produced by stress. Two examples may be given. In the first case, the head of newly amalgamated grammar and secondary modern schools appeared suddenly at the door of the crowded staff room at mid-morning break. He vigorously rang a miniature bell, bringing the noisy room to silence. He then harangued the staff about carelessness which might impair the school's reputation. A teacher had persistently accused a pupil of negligently losing a homework book. Finally, the parents had made representations in their son's defence. As a result, the Head had searched the classroom concerned and found the book. In the second case, the head of a middle school, after consultations with the teaching staff including the deputy-head, produced a modified timetable for the school. When the Head handed over a copy to the deputy-head for examination, the latter precipitately tore it into pieces and scattered them on the floor, shouting: 'It's no good, it won't do.'

Depicting structure – alternative forms

In trying to depict the structure of a school, teachers may find some satisfaction in using the pyramidal form, often called an organization chart. It provides certain information, but its limitations must be borne in mind. Among its deficiencies are the following:
- It cannot indicate the variation of work which an organization undertakes.
- No time-scale is given.
- It suggests only unidimensional and vertical relations.
- The versatility of individuals is concealed.

An alternative form of depicting structure is known as the matrix. It makes good some of these deficiences (Kingdon 1973). The use of the matrix presupposes a view of the task of the organization as ever-changing. Jobs, therefore, vary in duration, and may vary in kind. In teaching, it is not uncommon to find persons undertaking work that is quite different from that represented by their formal qualifications. It is true to say, however, that many forces in practice resist the level of organizational flexibility and personal adaptation which might be both desirable and attainable.

Where a fixed distribution of jobs, authority and positions is inappropriate and a variable structure is required, the matrix is a useful way of depicting the possibilities. Two fundamental ideas are necessary for devising a matrix.

1.   The total curricular programme for the school as a whole must be conceived as ongoing but separable into any desired number of sub-programmes or courses of varying duration.

2.   The total staff available are sub-divided on any desired basis for the purpose of discharging the sub-programmes as analysed.

Since both the curriculum of a school and the staff available to teach it are subject to change, it is possible to construct a matrix in two ways.

Fixed teams – variable programmes. In this form of the matrix, the staff are divided into teams with fixed membership. Each team subscribes its expertise to two or more sub-programmes at any one time. In those circumstances, the work that the team does is limited to the expertise it possesses. The pupil, because of the limited composition of a team, might be expected to be exposed to the teaching of more than one team.

Curricular programme for the school
sub-programme for pupil year groups

Teams	1	2	3	4
Mathematics				
Language				
Creative studies				
Investigational studies				

Figure 4.10 Example of matrix structure in a junior or middle school

In a school for the age-range 9–13 an example of structure in matrix form might be as follows. If only four teams comprehended all the curriculum between them, and the contribution of each was uniform throughout the school, the commitment of each team to each year group of pupils would be 25 per cent. In practice, all kinds of permutations may be considered and the final decisions entered in the boxes. For example, the Mathematics team might contribute 60 per cent of the work for 4, 20 per cent for 3, 10 per cent for 2 and 10 per cent for 1, whereas the Creative Studies team might contribute 20 per cent, 10 per cent, 10 per cent and 60 per cent respectively to the same pupil year groups. Language might then contribute 10 per cent, 10 per cent, 60 per cent and 20 per cent with Investigational Studies contributing 10 per cent, 60 per cent, 20 per cent and 10 per cent respectively.

The matrix could be further applied to the working of any one of these teams alone. If the team had four members, the individual teachers would replace the teams in the matrix. In each box could be shown the contribution made by each in respect of all four pupil year-groups. Indeed, a more detailed analysis of the sub-programme for each of the year-groups would be needed.

It may be noted that in schools where such teams are held to be omnicompetent and committed only to one year-group, the matrix is not needed. A simple pyramidal form is all that is required.

Fixed programmes – variable teams.   Being able to vary the composition of teams is a central consideration in using a matrix to depict structure, as shown in Fig. 4.11 for a secondary school. In this case, the sub-programmes may be conceived as relatively stable. The need is to form the very best teams possible and to vary the membership as necessary to maintain high standards or to bring to bear on a certain sub-programme the specialist contributions of a number of people. Each team would be subject to high-level overall leadership but various team members would lead the team's contribution to particular sub-programmes.

The total staff available
Variably formed teams according to need

Example Sub-programmes	1	2	3	4
Lower school combined studies				
CSE programme				
O Level programme				
A Level programme				

Figure 4.11 Example of a matrix structure in a secondary school

This particular matrix, if it applied to a secondary school, would imply two distinct differences from the traditional departmental structure. In the first place a team is specially formed for a purpose – to run a specific sub-programme. To do this it has far greater autonomy than that accorded to traditional departments. It is virtually an independent management unit. In the second place an individual teacher would be a member of different teams over a period of time, and a member of two teams simultaneously, perhaps, bearing in mind the need at all times to compose optimum teams in terms of balanced skills and cohesion.

In this example, Team I might give 60 per cent of its commitment to the 'A' Level programme, 20 per cent to the 'O' Level programme, 10 per cent to the CSE programme and 10 per cent to the Lower School Combined Studies programme. Teams 2, 3 and 4 would give complementary percentage contributions to make the complete programme viable.

The school as a complete organization

The forms used to depict the structure of a school should be capable of portraying the part or the whole. The examples given in this chapter so far have confined themselves to the teaching staff and their curricular and pastoral work. An inclusive analysis of the school as an extended organization, however, should take into account many more factors. The matrix may be used for this purpose, as demonstrated in Fig. 4.12, freely modified to allow the four sets of critical functions to be related. Inside the box, by means of different kinds of line, direct, indirect, strong and weak relations may be shown, not only as between groups, but also, if enough detail is added, between individuals. Under operational functions, on the north side of the box, Units 1, 2, etc. refer to teams, departments or any other identifiable sub-groups for getting the work of the school actually discharged.

Between them they encompass all the teaching functions whether conceived as instructional alone, or 'academic' and 'administrative' as separable functions. Individuals are grouped according to mutual interests, qualifications and programme demands. On the south side of the box are the support functions. There may be grouped on a similar

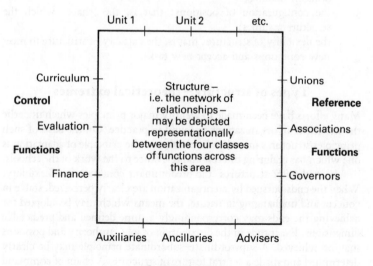

Figure 4.12 Matrix structure for depicting the inclusive functions of the school as an organization

basis all those whose organizational functions are of a second order, but are vitally necessary to the effective operation of the school. On the west side of the box may be listed those people whose function is regulatory, grouped according to the various spheres where control must be exercised over the operational life of the school. Some examples are given as the curriculum, evaluation (pupil, teacher and organizational performance) and finance. The head with various senior staff would be grouped for each of these. On the east side of the box are grouped people – some known, some unknown as individuals – who act as reference groups in different ways to the teaching and non-teaching staff of the school. The governors are a powerful known group. Professional or trades unions and subject or professional associations, though not generally in direct contact with a school, exercise normative influence by various means.

In thinking of the school in its entirety as an organization, six primary variables may be used to measure the structure and thus to make it possible to compare the structures of different schools (Pugh and Hickson 1976; Pugh and Hinings 1976; Paisey 1981).

1. the degree of specialization of function; that is, the division of work;
2. the degree of standardization of procedures; that is, the existence of rules;
3. the formalization of documentation; that is, the commitment of rules and other types of information to writing;
4. the degree of centralization of authority; that is, the location of decision making;
5. the configuration of positions; that is, the 'shape' which the structure assumes;
6. the flexibility of structure; that is, the capacity of structure to meet new conditions and accept new tasks.

Types of structure – theoretical extremes

Many efforts have been made to identify major principles which underlie the structures of organizations as found in practice. On the basis of such principles structures may then be classified. The principle of adaptation is one which has enduring interest and relevance to the work of the schools.

In *mechanistic* structures, the predominant condition is inflexibility. When the ends pursued by an organization are clearly perceived, stable in concept and unchanging in nature, the means which may be adopted for achieving the ends may correspondingly assume defined and predictable dimensions. Exactitude in the distribution of jobs, authority and positions may be achieved. A superordinate–subordinate principle may be clearly determined and made a central feature of structure. A chain of command binds the organization into a coherent, centrally directed whole. Communications pass through prescribed and orthodox channels. Initiative and diversity are minimized, since they are dispensed with by providing operating procedures for every eventuality.

In *organismic* or *organic* structures the opposite conditions prevail. The organization is conceived as trying to survive in constantly unstable and changing circumstances. At any point of time, the primary criterion for the distribution of jobs, authority and positions is making the best use of the human resources available, irrespective of precedence. The actual contributions of individuals and the pattern of interaction between individuals adopted must meet only the tests of possibility and suitability in relation to the task faced and the objectives set (Burns and Stalker 1968).

Mechanistic structure represents a closed value system. Organic structure represents an open value system.

It may be argued that the type of structure actually found in schools reflects 'internal' factors, like objectives, resources and preferences, but also 'external' factors like the school's historical development, providing body, location and size, level of independence and the kind of socio-economic community it serves.

Above all else, perhaps, structure is determined by the technology of the school – the characteristic way in which it undertakes its work, determined by the nature of the work itself. When a school is very small, the work is controlled by personal contact. Individuals know their jobs, authority and positions implicitly. People are usually flexible in their working methods. Typically, as the school grows, the personal, on-the-job control of the teaching gives way to control through 'specialists' in the organization who have singular status. With further growth, there is increasing direction and less discretion, control by more specialists and laid-down procedures. Finally, the school will reach a state of high specialization, or fine division of work, with many formalized procedures supported by codes of regulations. As discussed in Chapter 2, organization maintenance costs may have become excessive by this time. A new ideology may be necessary to provide a fundamentally different and more economic structure.

The structure of the school, as a result of human decision and action, should be seen in relation to the large and often ill-defined stock of ideas which inspire and guide community life in general. The values cherished by the community as a whole permit and constrain specific arrangements within organizations.

Size of organization is commonly a topic of concern and is often thought to be a critical variable in terms of engaging the 'whole person' in the work of the organization. Small organizations are often thought to be consistent with human happiness, efficiency and effectiveness. The criteria by which 'size' can be measured, however, vary and include numbers of people and financial and physical criteria such as the extent of buildings. Large organizations are often thought to be automatically malignant. The distinction should be drawn, however, between 'total' size and 'local' size. A multinational company may indeed be an enormous organization in total, but each operational sub-unit may be very small, intimate and satisfactory as a workplace.

By the same token, a school in total may seem of immense proportions, whatever criteria are adopted. This does not necessarily mean that such a school is a bad place to work in: a small school can be equally as bad. The structure adopted in any school needs to take account of the numbers of people involved, the task in hand, the technology adopted and the physical facilities and equipment available. Control, integration, flexibility and freedom from stress in an effective organization are the common objectives of all organizations, irrespective of size. Lack of understanding of alternative structures, or persistance with maladapted structures — as when there is great growth or great decline in the size of organization — are managerial deficiencies (Lambert 1979).

Organizational ideology and structure

Organizations cherish and demonstrate values in everything they do. Structure embodies prime values. Some of these values may be classified under the terms democracy, bureaucracy and federalism.

Democracy. Democracy is sometimes assumed to be an indivisible means for solving organizational problems. There are numerous definitions of democracy and in practice it is difficult to obtain consensus as to its meaning and application in precise situations. Democracy is concerned with ends in that the actual decisions made should result only from a decision-making process which is shared by all those who are to be affected by those decisions. Thus, the primary factors in democracy are participation and consent. An important corollary is the right to disagree. Recognition must be given, therefore, to the principle of dissent. Since dissent may be very inconvenient in practice, however, it may be tempting to employ coercive measures against dissenters. It is necessary, therefore, to accept dissent with impunity. Dissent is by definition a minority position. In democracy, the minority must be respected but the minority in turn is expected to observe the majority decision and to support its implementation.

As a consequence, decisions are made and practical problems are tackled in an open atmosphere of dialogue in which minority opinion forms and attempts to influence enough opinion to become itself the majority view. The size of schools and sheer physical problems of assembly, communication and consumption of time are potentially inimical to the practice of democracy. Ways to overcome the difficulties, however, may be found.

In direct democracy, all the people concerned must meet for discussion and to make decisions. Any member should be able to raise any matter and identify it as a problem. In other words, the concerns of one are potentially the concerns of all.

In representative democracy, the people concerned are too numerous to meet as a group. Representatives are nominated to act for the group. If this person has full powers vested in him, as a plenipotentiary, then he is empowered to make decisions which the group he represents will automatically accept. Such a person in this case must clearly be the choice of the group concerned.

A delegate, however, may be assigned by the group to represent its views but without power to commit it to any decision. Both the plenipotentiary and the delegate are accountable to the group, which retains the right to withdraw the office.

Democracy in procedural terms must cope with the different abilities of the members of the group and the varying degrees of willingness to lead and to take office. The principle of election in the group may be used to determine leadership or office on a permanent basis, a prescribed temporary basis, a regular basis subject to efficiency or on a shared basis in which positions are rotated with agreed time intervals.

Bureaucracy. Bureaucracy is often viewed as the antithesis of democracy. If democracy places more emphasis on ends in order to determine what the means should be, bureaucracy reverses the emphasis. It is preoccupied with order, logic and efficiency. The natural and ineradicable inequality of individuals is a fact which must lead to a hierarchical arrangement of rights and obligations. Decision emanates from one or few to many. The ability and right to identify issues which call for decision is the prerogative of one or few in any organization.

Organization members are not expected to conceive the organization as a whole. There are different levels of concern, at each of which decision-making is in limited hands. Decisions actually made are dependent on prior decision made at superordinate level and which, in turn, strictly affect those subsequently made at subordinate level. There is, therefore, a defined chain of command and communication. Jobs, authority and positions are prescribed, delegated and regulated.

Rules and procedures control all eventualities which may arise over the work to be done. In theory, novel events and problems should be anticipated at the very highest levels. In any case, novel circumstances should be referred from subordinate to superordinate levels. The division of labour is fine and the individual's concern is to maintain the *status quo*. Promotion is based upon his ability to do so rather than on eccentric flair and influence.

Like democracy, as a concept bureaucracy is not indivisible. It is identified in practice as a variable phenomenon, though in the past it was regarded as a homogeneous tool which would have to be used by all organizations in the modern technological society. Apologists have pointed out just how much has in fact been achieved by the application of bureaucracy, but have shown that variations in the modes of application can have varying effects – to the great harm as well as to the benefit of an organization (Gouldner 1955; Blau 1956).

Federalism. Federalism as a principle may be seen as lying mid-way between democracy and bureaucracy. It avoids the completely open position postulated by democracy in which decision-making is decentralized and the course of an organization is in theory unpredictable. It also avoids the directive approach and highly predictable outcomes sought in bureaucracy.

In an organization, participation is both possible and desirable in the making of decisions concerning some ends and some means. The possibility of constant, fundamental reappraisals generated by democracy and the inertia and potential maladaptability of bureaucracy are both avoidable. Flexibility and creativity can be secured by a process of deliberate and comprehensive decentralization. This is achieved by the constant and constitutional act of devolving responsibility from the centre to the periphery in an organization.

At the centre of the structure, the task of defining the nature of the organization's work is undertaken, together with an appraisal of the total and quality of resources available. In addition, the recruitment, induction and maintenance of the organization's membership is decided there. A small number of major prerogatives are, therefore, handled at the centre. The deployment of resources and the management of actual operations may then be fully devolved on sub-groups which, within the framework of possibilities created, are then deemed autonomous (Drucker 1962).

Summary

Organizational structure has been thought of as the distribution of jobs, authority and positions among the members of an organization. In a school, the structure may be regarded and depicted in two basic forms. The pyramidal form is a common way of representing structure. It articulates fixed positions and prescribed subordinate–superordinate relations, but does not provide for change. The matrix, in contrast, stresses the changing nature of the work and various combinations of staff which may be arranged to discharge it.

Structures in practice range between two extreme theoretical types. 'Mechanistic' structures are an adaptation to stable working conditions and tasks. 'Organismic' structures are adaptations to changing conditions and tasks. A way of measuring structure may consist of using six primary variables: specialization, standardization, formalization, centralization, configuration and flexibility.

The terms democracy, bureaucracy and federalism reflect different values. Each has a different bearing on the kind of structure a school might seek and the actual features which are adopted.

Discussion topics

1.   To what extent can a school be a democracy?

2. Evaluate the application of bureaucratic principles in the life of a school.

3. Identify examples of the application of federalist principles in current practice in the schools.

4. Compare the idea of autonomy for the teacher with the idea of learner-centred education. What kind of structure would a school need to cope with (a) each of these alone, and (b) both of these together?

Practical enquiry

Obtain diagrammatic statements of the staff structures of two primary and two secondary schools. Use contrasting schools if possible and invite such statements from the head of school and at least one other occupational category within each (e.g. assistant teacher, head of department, team-leader). Discuss and account for any differences of structure as between the types of school and between schools of the same type. Note and account for differences in the way that various staff from the same school depict the structure of their school.

5
MANAGING FOR RESULTS

Introduction

The idea of management is not restricted to formal organizations. It applies to the family, the nation, the international community and the human environment at large. When people speak of parents as being incompetent they usually mean that the parents manage their family affairs badly. Similarly the affairs of the national community can be either well or badly managed, as can relations between different national communities. In recent times people everywhere have become conscious of the fact that the common natural environment upon which the existence of the human species depends is itself subject to bad or good management.

Survival and order are characteristic notions embedded in all these cases, bearing in mind the need to think about the long-term future as well as the immediate. It is inadequate, however, to confine the meaning of management simply to a measure of success. There is the paradox that good management is exhibited in many conditions of apparent failure or disaster. The winding up of a company, a military retreat, a disaster at sea, a massive reduction in rail services or a widespread closure of pits in the coal-mining industry may all be well or badly managed.

If an adjective must be found to indicate the desirable state of management, that word is 'effective'. Management is human behaviour and it is effective when human needs embodied in objectives are met. In essence, therefore, management is the organizational process of formulating objectives, acquiring and committing the resources required to reach them and ensuring that the objectives are actually reached. It is a process of matching objectives and resources and is inevitably a *social* process. In this process objectives may have to be limited to the resources which are available or it may be necessary to procure resources to make it possible to attain the desired objectives. In this context 'good' management is obtaining exceptional results (objectives) with unexceptional resources − particularly if this is achieved in unpropitious circumstances.

Management and schools

The use of the term management in educational vocabulary is of comparatively recent origin. Its use has been controversial and sometimes acrimonious. The main reason for this is that the interpretations given to the word have been very limited and coloured by the meanings which people in education think are given to the word in manufacturing and commerce, and by the practice of management which they think exists there.

> The characterisation of the practice of management traditionally was in rather formal and simplistic terms and it is easier now to diagnose its limitations. It tended to be based on an inadequate understanding of individual and group behaviour, an insensitivity to social considerations, excessive division of labour, serious difficulties in the handling of authority relationships and in keeping a reasonable measure of control whilst not undermining the creative and initiating capacities of people. Newer thinking is providing better concepts for understanding the motivation and behaviour of people and for designing organizations in the light of this knowledge, an improved capacity to analyse and assess conflicting pressures, a greater acknowledgement of the factors of uncertainty and risk-taking in the policy and decision making responsibilities of management, a capacity to understand problems which cannot be neatly compartmented, a recognition that the integration of effort and activities is an infinitely more difficult yet more vital process than the processes of subdivision and specialisation. (Brodie 1979:1–2)

Reluctance to use the word management in education accompanies a reluctance to apply the concepts and techniques of management, according to some observers. A pessimistic view, for example, has been expressed in the following way: 'Further Education Principals know about management ... Heads of secondary schools, especially ambitious ones, also know a bit about management ... Primary Heads do not. ...' (Taylor 1975:4)

Because of the various meanings which attach to the word management, misunderstandings may arise. In the following passage, particular areas which are the concern of management together with some of the inadequacies which may be perceived in current practice are identified.

> ... the proposition is that management is a missing dimension in education. The school is a social institution of particular subtlety and sensitivity. The individual teacher has all the pressures which come from working in a situation largely not of his or her own making ... There are large distances, organisational and psychological, between the teacher and others who make up the larger educational system. Timetabling and other day-to-day demands squeeze out the time

and often the energy and motivation to give adequate thought to the longer term. Preoccupation with subject curricula and examinations takes priority over questions of policy, organisation and resources. Objectives and priorities are left implicit and not matters for the intimate involvement of staff. The interaction of a school with its environment is often ambiguous. Autonomy, which should bring with it a sense of freedom to initiate and experiment, turns too readily to insularity and conservatism. Tensions which ought to be productive of open debate and of creative development may be left unresolved with relationships at arms-length. (Brodie 1979:3)

Management is concerned with both objective and subjective phenomena. A great deal of the misunderstanding in education arises because people think of management as being concerned *only* with the objective – with measuring output and being accountable on the basis of measurable results. That this is only part of the matter is well illustrated in the following passage.

Because management deals with human beings, it can never be completely scientific, and must be regarded partly as an art. The reason for this is that while scientific techniques are applied to materials governed by known physical laws, the techniques of management are applied to people and must rely on people to ensure that they are properly applied. They can only be successfully applied by someone who has learned to understand people by experience of dealing with them. (International Labour Office 1964:26)

Management involves values, attitudes, techniques and behavioural patterns at both strategic and tactical levels. All these, however, do not constitute an indivisible whole which may be either accepted or rejected. They are varying in nature and are as much a part of the infinite variety of reality as anything else. Different types of organization call for different types of management, different situations within a particular organization require specific skills. The realization that organization in education should be properly managed is incumbent on everyone, as stated in the following quotation.

Management and its techniques are applicable at all levels of the educational service and I mean *all levels* because it doesn't matter whether you are a class teacher or head of department, or a head teacher or an administrative officer in local government or even a civil servant, there are management techniques which are appropriate to your particular sphere of activity. (Brooksbank 1972:9)

It is reasonable to differ over the *quality* of management which is exercised but there can be no question about the *existence* of management and the *need* for it in educational institutions. Wherever there is organization there is management. Management is to organization as the skin is to the body. In practical terms, schools share the fate of other organizations in adult life. Some are well managed: they are judged useful for social purposes and their members enjoy their membership of the organizations concerned as a way of spending their working life. Some are badly managed: they are judged harshly because their work is of ill-repute and their members are alienated or even hostile. Every conceivable gradation between these two extremes may be found.

The questions of management

Management is complex human activity whether the viewpoint is that of an individual person in action or that of a group of people in action as a management team. Many attempts to classify all the behaviour involved have been made. All of them are concerned to analyse the functions which are necessary if an organization is to survive and prosper. An example of such an analysis is that of planning, regulating, commanding, coordinating, controlling and evaluating (Urwick 1963). In essence, however, management is being concerned with a series of simple but unavoidable questions, which apply equally when the scale of organization and the resources used is large as well as small. These questions may be arranged as follows.

PURPOSE	**What** is done?
	Why is it done?
	What **else** might be done?
	What **should** be done?
PLACE	**Where** is it done?
	Why is it done **there**?
	Where **else** might it be done?
	Where **should** it be done?
SEQUENCE	**When** is it done?
	Why is it done **then**?
	When **might** it be done?
	When **should** it be done?
PERSON	**Who** does it?
	Why does **that** person do it?
	Who **else** might do it?
	Who **should** do it?
MEANS	**How** is it done?
	Why is it done **that** way?
	How **else** might it be done?
	How **should** it be done?

(International Labour Office 1978:101–20)

The answer to these questions and the ways and means used to find them will vary between schools. The history, size, type and catchment area of the school are some of the variables which affect the particular answers given. Over time, new answers to the old questions must be found and this requires ability, effort and constant vigilance. Management work is demanding. The school which runs smoothly may convey the misleading impression that it is easy work, whereas the school which moves from crisis to crisis may create the impression that good management is impossible to achieve.

Documents based on these simple questions have been offered by some Local Education Authorities to schools in their areas to help them to take a broad, systematic and continuous view of their work. A pioneering and exhaustive example of one of these documents states that it is the purpose of the document to provide 'an aid to teachers individually or collectively, and schools in examining the value of what they do ... a starting point for discussion and further questioning whenever a school as a whole, or a department within a school, considers it appropriate to take stock of what it is achieving.' (Oxfordshire County Council 1979:3)

School management models

The scope and task of management in the school are represented in the two models which follow. In the first of these the range of necessary skills in the individual is analysed and the major areas to which they may be applied are identified. This may be called the Applied Skills Model, presented as Fig. 5.1. In this model *conceptual skills* are those of comprehensive understanding, the ability to integrate all the elements involved, the ability to perceive possibilities and to relate events to higher order principles. *Technical skills* are those of 'know-how', the possession of information, motor and behavioural competences, knowledge of procedures and the constraints and resources which govern the work of a

Individual skills \ Applied fields	Educational	External relations	Finance and facilities	Staff development
Conceptual				
Human				
Technical				

Figure 5.1 School management model based on individual skills and applied fields (Adapted from a talk by W. Taylor, 'A Working Partnership', BBC Radio, 1970)

school together with specific techniques. *Human skills* are those of being able to encourage people to give their best efforts to the organization, to create a healthy climate of working conditions, to introduce changes without losing morale and to communicate clearly and in such a manner as to create confidence.

All these skills are needed and may be exhibited in each of the four applied fields. The *educational* field includes the curricular programme, its objectives, syllabus content and coordination, and the teaching methods and techniques employed. The field of *external relations* includes creating and sustaining a favourable image of the school in the minds of parents, the media, the many agencies which have an interest in the school, local government officers and other officials, and local firms and bodies which may be of service to the school. The field of *finance and facilities* covers all the non-human resources which are available to the school, particularly the use of plant. The field of *staff development* includes the matching of person to job, performance evaluation, redeployment and the progressive increase of staff competences.

The second model of management in the school turns on the notion of the range of decisions which must be made and the patterns of participation by which they are made. This may be called the Participation Model, presented as Fig. 5.2.

The nominated items under *decision areas* represent a set of categories for sorting all the decisions which are made in the course of managing the school. They are derived from conceptualizing the complete spectrum of decisions which a school must make. Suitable analytical divisions of this spectrum are then made and appropriately labelled. This particular set is not inviolable but is an attempt to encompass every conceivable decision. This means that the labels must be interpreted broadly.

'Curriculum content' covers decisions to choose and reject the content of the learning programme. This includes subject identification on the academic side but also decisions on questions of an inter-disciplinary approach, project activity and individualized programmes, insofar as learning method and experience become content, and the materials to be used for teaching the chosen content.

'Educational objectives' are thought of as changes hoped for in the pupils as a result of having followed the programme offered by the school – including the process of defining these changes, modifying them, publishing them or, in short, arriving at any shared, explicit conclusion or statement about what the work of the school is for.

'Evaluation' indicates the area of decision concerned with the design of pupil record cards, the extent of pupil records, the kind of coverage they should have and the choice of any diagnostic and/or predictive tests to be used. This category also includes procedures to be adopted by the teachers and questions such as the accessibility of various parties to the records. Finally, it embraces all decisions regarding measures of teacher performance and organizational effectiveness, together with decisions on the procedures and arrangements for making use of them.

Participation Levels / Decision Areas	Decisional deprivation	Decisional equilibrium	Decisional saturation
Curriculum content			
Educational objectives			
Evaluation			
External relations			
Finance			
Pupil grouping			
Staffing			
Teaching methods/ techniques			
Timetabling/ use of plant			
Use of materials/ equipment			

Figure 5.2 School management model based on decision areas and participation levels (Paisey 1981)

'External relations' includes all contacts for whatever purpose with a parent or guardian in connection with the pupil's work, relationships or conduct and condition. This includes documentary contact such as the sending of written information and reports, replying to letters, and requesting parental visits to school for advisory or consultative purposes. In addition, this category includes all decisions about relations with external bodies of all kinds, the local authority, the mass media and the school's neighbours.

The decision area labelled 'finance' refers to the discretionary monies available to the school. It includes questions of disbursement — the actual amounts which individuals or groups receive, whether or not this is paid in a lump sum for autonomous expenditure, and whether or not any direction is attached to agreed grants. This decision area also involves minor works alterations to the plant and the purchase of equipment and machinery for use at school level. In short, this category is concerned with all incoming and outgoing monies in various forms, uses to which they are put and procedures for handling them.

The category 'pupil grouping' stands for the complete process of sub-grouping of the total pupil population of the school, together with group recompositions and modifications. It includes the bases for sub-groupings, their size and degree of permanence and the level of discretion over sub-sub-grouping by the individual teacher, teaching team, department or faculty.

'Staffing' includes appointments, deployment, promotions, retraining and development, working hours, the assignment of student teachers and all matters to do with the adult members of the organization as employees, insofar as they lie within the powers of discretion afforded to the school.

'Teaching methods/techniques' involves how the individual teacher or teaching team goes about his or its work. It includes the division of labour between teachers, the type of division of labour between teacher and pupil and between pupils, and the regulatory behaviour employed by the staff. This also includes questions of quality, quantity, sequence and pace of the pupil's work, the particular way chosen to teach a particular content and coping with learning difficulties and indiscipline.

'Timetabling/use of plant' stands for the adopted programme of activities or learning experiences and involves the allocation of plant and facilities, the amount of time devoted to any particular unit of curriculum, the times when rooms and facilities may be used, the use that may actually be made of them, subsequent changes in their use and what plant and facilities are permanently allocated or rationed on a time basis.

The 'use of materials/equipment' refers to consumable and non-consumable items needed for teaching purposes by teachers and/or the pupils. Questions of kind, quality and quantity are included, as are questions of storage, mode of distribution and actual usage.

The term *participation* in the model refers to the amount of decision-making which individuals are empowered to undertake. It is not uncommon to hear assertions that one person — notably the head of school — makes all the decisions. Such assertions are patently unfounded. It is true, however, that some decisions are more important and far reaching for the life of the school than others. These decisions often remain in the hands of the head of school or in the hands of a few members of the teaching staff. Given such a list of decision areas in the model, it is possible to assign an order of priority to each in terms of its strategic importance to the overall life of the school. Furthermore, it is possible for individuals in the organization to assess the amount of say which they feel they have in each area. This will reveal either a state of satisfaction or *decisional equilibrium*, a state of unsatisfied demand or *decisional deprivation*, or a state of overwork or *decisional saturation* (Alutto and Belasco 1972).

Members of an organization experience a sense of either
decisional deprivation
(desired participation is in excess of actual participation)
or
decisional equilibrium
(desired participation and actual participation are equal)
or
decisional saturation
(actual participation is in excess of desired participation)

Original authority lies with the person appointed as head of school. One of the most important manifestations and applications of this authority is to decide on the levels of participation which the school as an organization shall have. In general, the head may strive for high or low levels of participation. In addition, high levels of participation may be confined to a small proportion of staff or extended to all. These levels may apply to all decision areas or only to some of them. The actual pattern of participation deriving from the interplay of all these variables in a particular school forms the basis for a staff development policy and obviously a point of departure for a management strategy to increase or reduce the extent of decision-making powers.

In schools which have intermediate authority levels, such as team leaders, heads of department and heads of year groups, the participation policy favoured by the head of school may or may not be faithfully reflected within the sub-organization – though generally in teaching, as elsewhere, 'people lower down tend to take their attitudes from the man at the top' (International Labour Office 1978:38).

The ability and willingness to work in accordance with the general policy is of course a factor governing the selection of teachers for middle management positions in many schools. Some schools prefer to have a homogeneous character for their organization in regard to participation, leaning either to restricted or to extended levels of participation. Others may deliberately choose to be heterogeneous, in which case sub-organizations are allowed to run their affairs in their own way.

As the foregoing considerations imply, it is a fact that people differ in the ways in which they want to approach their managerial tasks. Heads of schools and senior teachers in all kinds of positions exhibit different behaviour as they go about their work. The principles underlying these differences are important and have differential effects on organizational performance. Personal behaviour in managerial work is known as management 'style'.

Sharing management work

It is far too simplistic to think that the larger the school the greater the amount of management activity and the higher the level of difficulty. A director of education has queried the widely held assumption '... that the smallest institutions with least resources and supporting colleagues are easiest to manage' (Taylor 1975:4).

To a considerable extent the amount of management work required is in the hands of the organization itself. A small school may be highly complex as an organization and require a great deal of managing. A large school may be less complex as an organization and require less managing. In both cases the volume of management activity required may be undertaken by one person or few, or it may be shared widely. If a school is organized in a less complex way it may be possible for the head of school or a few senior staff to undertake all the important managerial behaviour, though it may be undesirable for them to do so. For one person or few to manage a complex organization, however, is really a contradiction of terms. More complexity means more interpersonal transactions, the sheer volume of which needs a broader or decentralized management base.

The process of delegation is an inevitable consequence of finite human capacity facing the extending complexity of organization. The infinite welter of stimuli which clamour for attention in organizations must be limited, filtered and shared. At any point in time the experience and ability of each member enables him to share a certain part of the organization's total burdens but this part is limited for every individual. Each is unable to respond to additional stimuli beyond a certain limit.

The occurrence of overstimulation leads to organizational stress. This condition is commonplace and in recent years has become subject to intensive study (Kahn *et al.* 1964; Frankl 1967; Wright 1975; Coleman 1976; Cooper and Marshall 1978; Melhuish 1978; Woolfolk and Richardson 1979). The pervasive and deleterious effects of organizational stress, as well as the costs involved, imply that management has a serious responsibility to structure organizations in ways which minimize the incidence of it as far as possible. The dimensions of this responsibility are well articulated in the following passage.

> No head can exercise leadership without delegating most of his responsibilities. But he may delegate in a number of ways. He may delegate responsibility but not the power; he may delegate the task but not the power; he may delegate the power but not the accountability. In each of these cases his delegation would be

dysfunctional in that the teacher would not be able to perform the
delegated task fully and would remain in a state of subordination or
dependency which would be restrictive of future initiatives. A more
useful management concept is that of collaboration or sharing –
which is true 'delegation'. Collaboration involves total sharing of
responsibilities which includes the right to succeed and to fail. There
can be no real sharing (delegation) if the right to fail is not also shared
(delegated) since anything less is incomplete and cannot be said to be
true sharing (delegation). A head who does not share (delegate) the
right to fail may be retaining control over the situation but he cannot
be said to be showing full respect for and confidence in his
colleagues. A vital consideration for all managers is the extent to
which they dare share their responsibilities – the assumption being
that the stronger the individual the more he will risk. Generally
speaking managers are paid to take risks even if they are calculated
ones. Unless responsibilities and power are shared among the
members the organisation will lack creativity and adaptability. If
schools are to be open, creative and supportive institutions for the
pupils, they must be so for the teachers also. (Gray 1979b:63)

Two special points about delegation need to be made. In the first
place, it must be emphasized that delegation should be conceived as a
continuous process. The *volume* of responsibilities which may be involved
is always changing in total. The *kind* of responsibilities which may be
subject to delegation over a period of time may change significantly in
nature. Above all, however, the volume and kind of responsibilities
which a particular individual at any particular time is asked to bear may
be *decreased* as well as increased. Responsibilities may cease or may be
moved from one person to another.

The second point concerns the fact that delegation is nearly always
thought about as a hierarchical function. Delegation is often restricted in
organizational thinking to the right and duty which a 'superordinate' or
boss may exercise in relation to a 'subordinate'. The process of delegation
at heart is a process of sharing management work. When a collegial –
rather than a single hierarchical – principle governs the relationships
between organization members, the process of sharing may be initiated
by many people, all of whom may find themselves at the head of a
hierarchy according to different task allocations and different
circumstances. Thus, the 'subordinate' in one set of circumstances or for
one particular task may be the 'superordinate' in another. This
consideration underlies the final sentence in the passage quoted above.

Of the main zones of concern to those who manage the school, the
academic and teaching zone involving the teaching staff is inevitably
managed on a broad basis, through faculties, departments, year groups or
teams, and individual teachers who have considerable autonomy in what
they do and how they respond to the ever changing pattern of the school
day. The involvement of teaching staff in the other zones of school life

away from the immediate instructional and disciplinary situation, however, is a matter of great variability from school to school.

It is often forgotten that the non-teaching staff of a school are also members of the organization. They too are potentially able to undertake varying degrees of involvement in deciding on courses of action and helping to shape the kind of organization to which they belong.

> In all institutions little or no regard seems to be given to the views of the non-teaching staff. Their influence on policy is usually through the greater or lesser degree of co-operation with which they are prepared to receive the decisions of others. Yet the administrative, caretaking, clerical and catering staff can often be as large as the teaching staff and in ensuring the well-being and effectiveness of the community, as important. (Taylor 1975:5)

Management stress

An important responsibility in management work is to obtain an organizational structure which will avoid or minimize stress in organization members. Above all, however, individuals who are in management positions should remember that they too are organization members, equally prone but exceptionally exposed to organizational stress and its ravages. Perhaps mindful of the self-neglect which they might have, one Local Education Authority has formally asked heads of schools to ask themselves from time to time the following question: 'Are some clerical and administrative tasks delegated to members of staff on a regular basis?' (Oxfordshire County Council 1979:7)

This question to heads of schools is supplemented by its natural corollaries: 'How accurate is my awareness of the load carried by different individual teachers?' and 'How accurate is my awareness of the load carried by non-teaching staff?' (Oxfordshire County Council 1979:8)

These questions need to be asked and answered since it seems that teaching may be particularly hazardous to one's health. The conditions of stress which have been found to be characteristic in teaching have been identified as follows.

> 'A reaction of the nervous system to stress, leading to a variety of physical diseases.'
> 'A disruption of personal or professional life as a result of occupational stress.'
> 'Destructive feelings of emotional stress as a result of ineffective coping?
> 'Loss of concern and detachment from those with whom you work.'
> 'A cynical and dehumanized perception of pupils, accompanied by a deterioration of the quality of teaching.'
>
> (Walsh 1979:253)

Management work in most organizations across the spectrum of occupations is generally regarded as demanding. Management work in the teaching profession, therefore, may be regarded as being potentially doubly hazardous. The sources of stress for people in educational management positions have been identified as follows:

> 'The feeling that you have too little authority to carry out responsibilities assigned to you.'
> 'Being unclear on just what the scope and responsibilities of your job are.'
> 'Feeling that you have too heavy a work load, one that you can't possibly finish during an ordinary work day.'
> 'Thinking that you are not able to satisfy the conflicting demands of various people over you.'
> 'Feeling that you are not fully qualified to handle the job.'
> 'Feeling you are unable to influence your immediate supervisor's decisions and actions that affect you.'
> 'Feeling that you have to do things on the job that are against your better judgement.'
>
> (Wheeler 1971:3)

The scope of school management

The scope of managerial responsibility for a school is formally defined in general terms by the Local Education Authority and is initially vested in the head of school, who remains formally accountable to the authority irrespective of the kind of managerial strategy which he or she decides to adopt to create a working organization. The following are two varying examples of the legal and administrative basis on which the authority of the head of school rests.

Berkshire Education Authority. County Primary Schools, Nursery, Special and Secondary Schools. (Included under the heading 'Organisation and Curriculum'.)

> The Headteacher shall be responsible to the Governors for the general direction of the conduct and curriculum of the school. Subject to the provisions of these Rules/Articles, the Headteacher shall control the internal organisation, management and discipline of the school and shall exercise supervision over the teaching and non-teaching staff. (Berkshire County Council 1979b:2)

Hampshire Education Authority. County Primary Schools in the age-range 2–12, Secondary Schools and Secondary Colleges. (Included under the heading 'Organisation'.)

> Subject to the provisions of these Rules the Head shall be professionally responsible to the Governors for the internal organisation, management, curriculum, and discipline, of the school, and for the supervision of the teaching and non-teaching staff. (Hampshire Education Committee 1976:17; 1977:23)

Apart from the academic and teaching zone of the school, there is the vast array of events and business matters which make up the total life of the school as an organization. This is the zone of internal systems and procedures which make the existence of a densely crowded institution tolerable and productive. This is the zone of school life beyond the classroom where management particularly applies. Schools possess varying degrees of autonomy for deciding their own affairs in this zone of general management of the school, but must always meet certain legal and administrative requirements in addition. These are promulgated by the local education authority and may be sometimes regarded as onerous and irksome to the schools. In the London area, for example, research reported in 1974 revealed that there was widespread dissatisfaction with the administrative superstructure among heads of schools. They felt that none of the parties involved really understood the conditions and problems at operational level. Attitudes displayed not only included despair but distrust and even contempt (Steinman 1974).

Schools often wish for greater freedom of action and flexibility. Some people think that the mass of conventions which characterize school life are a bar to making the school a more effective and attractive place to be in.

The nine-month school year, the five-day week, the seven-hour day, the forty-five minute period – these are all conventions. You do not need that particular set of conventions to have a school, any more than you need bad food to have a prison ... as things stand now – for us, in this time and place – the institution known as school, for all of its irritating, even preposterous, defects, does not appear to be in jeopardy of crumbling ... the most realistic hope of improving school lies in modifying its conventions, not its essential functions. (Postman and Weingartner 1973:22–3)

The framework of rules, procedures and guidance issued by a Local Education Authority is invariably substantial. Within this framework – which at once provides a set of constraints and thereby defines a set of opportunities – the operational management of the school is conducted. The various rules and items of guidance and procedural requirements which together make up the administrative provisions for a school may be drawn together as a handbook. This may be modified and updated from time to time as necessitated by changes in the law or changes in financial or other areas of local government policy concerning education.

By implication, the handbooks of administrative documents issued to schools show the nature and extent of the managerial work which must be undertaken to keep a school at a level of operational effectiveness. Two examples of classified subjects on which Local Education Authorities give advice, issue directives or provide information in documentary form, are given as follows.

Example 1 Berkshire Education Authority

Accounting

(a) General provisions for all county institutions
Income
Expenditure
Security
Petty cash accounts
Salaries and wages
Insurances
Miscellaneous

(b) Specific provisions in addition for schools
School meals income
Sales – craftwork, cookery, etc.
Lettings
Hire of musical instruments
Miscellaneous income
Special activities allowance
Heads' out-of-pocket expenses
Travelling expenses of teachers
'Out-county' and pool pupils
School journeys

(Berkshire County Council 1979a)

Organization

General
Advisory service
Careers service
Child guidance clinic – school psychological service
Education welfare officers
Further education/adult education
Library resources service
Education catering service
School health service
County youth and community service

The pupil

Nursery education
First admission to infants schools
Transfer from infant to junior schools
(or from first to middle schools)
Transfer from primary to secondary education
Leaving school
Out county/no area pupils
Financial assistance
● Maintenance allowances
● Vacation, field study and special courses

- Clothing grants
  (a) Free meals
  (b) School meals debts
- Assistance towards fees at independent schools
- Boarding awards
- Major awards and grants
- Higher education interview expenses

Special schools and handicapped pupils
Home teaching
School attendance
Transport to and from school
Irregular school attendance
Employment of children
Registration and admission of pupils from overseas
Individual pupil records

Staff

Teaching staff
- General conditions of appointment
- Resignation
- Payment of salary
- Medical certificates
- Absence from duty
- Attendance at courses
- Security of employment – dismissal and redundancy

Ancillary staff
Trade unions and labour relations
Legislation

School administration

School registers and records
- Admission register
- Attendance register
- Punishment book
- School annals

Curriculum, religious worship and instruction
School term and holiday dates
Dress
Discipline and punishment
- Detention
- Corporal punishment
- Exclusion
- Suspension

Wilful damage by children in school premises
Safety at school
- Supervision
- Fire precautions
- Explosive devices

- Accidents and sudden illness
Non-accidental injury to children of any age
Educational visits
Ordering of goods and services
Health and safety at work
Premises, repairs and maintenance, lettings
Returns

Insurance
General
Fire
Pressure plant, lifts and other machinery
Motor vehicles
Money
Employer's liability
Fidelity guarantee
Assault
Personal accident (employees and voluntary)
Teachers engaged on out of school activities
School journeys abroad
Work experience schemes
Public liability
Further information
(Berkshire Education Committee 1979)

Example 2 Hampshire Education Authority

Sites and Buildings
Fire precaution
Illegal entries
Maintenance and improvement works to school buildings
Vehicular damage to school property
Window cleaning

Finance
Security of cash
Petty cash
School general allowances
Private school funds
Teachers' removal expenses
Travelling expenses scheme and subsistence allowances
Telephones
School mini-buses and coaches

Supplies, equipment and requisitions
How supplies are obtained
How to pay for supplies
Supplies chargeable to central funds

Establishment and entitlement to staff
- Teachers
  - Basic staffing ratios
  - Posts of responsibility
- Ancillary staff
- Caretakers/cleaners
- School meals

Appointments
- Teachers
  - Authority to appoint
  - Appointments to scale posts
  - Procedures for reducing teacher allocation
  - Appointment to area teaching staff
  - Probationary teachers
  - Relief teachers
- Ancillary staff
  - Authority to appoint
  - Recommendation of appointment
  - Redeployment
- Caretakers/cleaners
- School meals

The staff

Advertising
- Teachers
  - internal
  - external
- Others

Accidents

Leave of absence
- Teachers
  - sickness
  - maternity
  - other than sickness
  - jury service
- Ancillary staff
  - sickness and maternity
  - other than sickness
- Caretaking and school meals staff
  - sickness and maternity
  - other than sickness

Contracts of employment
- Job description
- Notice periods

Courses and training
Disciplinary procedure
Grievance procedure
Removal expenses
Resignations

Retirement
> Age of retirement
> Premature retirement of teachers

Salaries/wages
Teachers' associations and the county council
> Relationships between them

The pupils

Admissions
> Standard procedures
> Exceptional procedures

School leaving dates
Transport
> Pupils attending designated schools
> Pupils attending other than designated schools

Grants
> Free school meals
> Free milk
> Uniform and maintenance grants for secondary school pupils
> Grants for extra-curricular activities

Non-accidental injury
Accidents to pupils
Corporal punishment
Detention
Suspension
Special education
> Assessment and placement
> Pre-school age handicapped children
> Handicapped children in the ordinary school
> Home tuition

School uniform

(Hampshire Education Committee 1979)

External responsibilities

As indicated above, the task of management is to maintain the academic and teaching zone and also a systems and procedures zone for the school. These are internal. In addition it must be ready to meet the repercussions for the school which are generated by policies, opinions or actions adopted, expressed and taken by external bodies. Items in this zone of external effects may attract public attention and become the subject of controversy in the mass media. They give rise to an added dimension of managerial responsibility in the school – the need to shape, develop and protect the school's public image. Some examples of this are as follows.

In the first example, rumours had circulated that a large number of the teaching staff of a secondary school were planning to leave the school owing to their dissatisfaction with the internal management of the school. Parents believed that about a third of the teaching staff were leaving because they were 'being told how to teach'. The head of school allegedly held 'a very tight rein' over the staff and what went on at the school, fears being expressed that such changes were bound to have a detrimental effect on the education of the pupils (*Reading Chronicle* 1979).

One of the singular concerns of school management is that of security. Schools have commonly become prey to arsonists, vandals and thieves. The two following examples – one from primary, the other from secondary, education – were taken from the same edition of a local newspaper (*Reading Chronicle* 1979).

Primary school. Callous thieves have betrayed the trust of pupils and teachers at a Reading school. During last Saturday's fete ... 'the wall carving disappeared ... while the school was very busy. All the doors were open and anyone could have taken the carving. We did think about moving the thing but it's very sad if you can't trust people for even one day.'

Secondary school. The fire which destroyed a storage hut at ———— Comprehensive School on Saturday was 'obviously started deliberately' according to the headmaster. The hut, a small timber building set apart from the school, caught fire at about 10 pm. Within 20 minutes the structure was burnt to the ground. 'It was lucky the wind was blowing away from the school. Windows along workshops near the hut have been cracked by the heat. If the wind had been coming from the east the whole school might have caught fire.'

Local Education Authorities inevitably create managerial problems for the head and the staff of schools when significant changes of policy are introduced. Such changes may arise from a variety of causes but none so potent as the need to make outright financial economies, such as in the following example.

Drastic cuts in education are being considered by Kent County Council. They include: A five per cent cut in heating, on top of the five per cent imposed last year. A 10 per cent cut in manpower. Teachers are included in the cuts as are cleaners and secretaries but senior caretakers and senior secretaries are exempt. ... A continuous working day to enable schools to close at 2.30 p.m. ... Switching the long summer holiday to the winter to save on heating costs. (*Isle of Thanet Gazette* 1979)

Decisions taken by the Local Education Authority may not only create the need for extended management activity in the school, as in the case of substantial financial economies, but also cause the school to attract unjustified local misunderstanding and hostility, as in the following case:

> ... School will be closed for three days this term for different
> elections, and although the children will be pleased, their parents are
> up in arms.
>
> The headmaster said: 'I cannot understand why they cannot hold
> the three elections together, and I have made my objections to the
> local authority and the returning officer. I have done my best to
> change it, but I have been told that this is their decision. What
> concerns me is that people seem to think I am responsible in some
> way for the arrangement of the general election. But I just do as I am
> told by the education committee, and elections have been held at the
> school for about 70 years.' (*The Henley Standard* 1979a)

Developments in ideas about the place of the school in the local
community as well as economic and financial considerations have led to
changes in the use of school buildings. The 'multi-option' or 'variable-
use' school is emerging (Ader 1975). The extended use of school buildings
both in terms of time beyond the normal school day and in terms of
activity beyond those of the usual scholastic kind, places additional
management responsibilities on the school. These may be indirect and
negative in many cases – suffering the dislocations or after effects such as
broken equipment – as well as direct, in the sense of needing to
coordinate the extended uses to which school plant is put. The following
report is evidence of the trend.

> [the] County Council is encouraging the public to 'share' schools
> with the education department by using the premises out of school
> hours. Five thousand copies of a leaflet have been produced to set out
> the council's policy of aiming to get the fullest possible use from the
> millions of pounds invested in school buildings. ...
>
> The leaflet also gives details of the council's policy on joint
> provision ... and joint extension schemes where a school building is
> enhanced to make it more suitable for community use. (*The Henley
> Standard* 1979b)

A large number of auxiliary and related professions have developed
in education during recent years. Many of these have direct access to
schools and others have relationships which are still being defined.
Liaison with such bodies is a further responsibility placed upon school
management where boundaries and tasks await clearer definition, as
illustrated in the following quotation.

> The theme of the Conference has been selected to meet what is felt to
> be a growing need for the Youth and Community Service to
> consider the future of the Service in relation to schools, and, in
> particular, the increasing use of the term 'Community School' and
> the creation of Departments of Community Education. There is also
> the need to clarify the roles of the increasing band of people, known

as Youth Tutors, Teacher/Leaders, Community Workers, Adult/ Youth Tutors, Youth and Community Workers, Heads of Community Education, Heads of Social Education, and others who are working within the secondary school system. There are also many Youth and Community Workers who at present have little or no connection with secondary schools, who are anxious about their future role in the Service and their relationships both with the secondary schools in the locality where they work and also with their colleagues who work within the school. (National Association of Youth Service Officers 1974)

Many other events outside the school pose managerial problems within it. Industrial action by teachers, added to seemingly higher teacher absenteeism (Bamber 1979) as well as industrial action in other industries and shortages of fuel and other materials, make the work of managing the school more demanding. The distracting, absorbing and dislocating effects of these factors are made abundantly clear in the following extracts.

> Schools ... are faced with more industrial action by teachers who are angry over a decision to dock wages ...
> ... From Monday morning, nearly 1,000 teachers, all members of the National Association of Schoolmasters/Union of Women Teachers, will just work the normal school timetable.
> Before- and after-school activities will be stopped and no lunch-time supervision will be done. This is just the first stage of action ...
> ... In most cases teachers were packing up work 20 to 30 minutes before school officially closed ...
> ... Councillors were warned of the action yesterday by the secretary of (the county's) biggest teaching union, the National Union of Teachers.
> Schools had already suffered enough disruption (said a representative).
> Bad weather, oil shortages, elections, the NUPE strike and teachers' action had forced them to close.
> 'The public, teachers and parents are sick to death with action in these schools.'
> 'This council is knowingly provoking more industrial action by implementing such a petty, punitive measure,' he said. (*Henley Mercury* 1979)

Management style

Management style has been briefly defined as the chosen strategy of an individual which he tends to repeat. In referring to the managerial behaviour of individuals in organizations, confusion between the terms 'strategy' and 'style' may arise. This confusion may be avoided, however, if a distinction is made between the two on the basis of the *intentions* of the individual manager concerned. The term 'strategy' is best reserved for the behavioural pattern which the individual chooses, implements and sustains in order to achieve the qualitative results he seeks. The term 'style' is best reserved for the impact *actually made on others*. Thus, 'style' is the visible aspect of strategy and depends upon the perceptual capacities of the receiver or observer of the managerial behaviour exhibited. The management style of a senior teacher, therefore, is the assessment made by colleagues in a particular work setting, based on sufficient observations of his working in a variety of circumstances (Paisey and Paisey 1980).

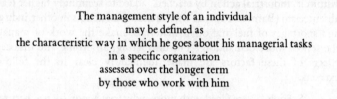

The management style of an individual
may be defined as
the characteristic way in which he goes about his managerial tasks
in a specific organization
assessed over the longer term
by those who work with him

Since management is concerned in the final analysis with what organization members *are* doing, what they *might* be doing and what they *should* be doing, it is axiomatic that the basis of management is a set of general assumptions about people in organizations. These have been codified under two heads. The first set, known as 'Theory X', is pessimistic in tone. Those who take a 'Theory X' position expect little from the generality of people in terms of creative capacity, ability to make intelligent decisions, reliability and hard work without the application of sanctions. The second set, known as 'Theory Y', is optimistic in tone. Those who take a 'Theory Y' position expect much from others, believing in their creative capacity, participative willingness and potential, reliability and application to work, given the right contextual conditions in the organization (McGregor 1960; 1967). It has been argued that the variable adoption of 'Theory X' and 'Theory Y' behaviour is possible and that it might be desirable in order to be fully adaptive. This formula has been named 'Theory Z' (Simmons 1971) and may be applied in organizations at three levels – at the level of the individual, at the level of the sub-group and at the level of the organization as a whole.

One manifestation of 'Theory X' is seen in the autocratic behaviour of the individual who enforces his own pre-determined decision by manipulative means which compel alienative or calculative responses in others. Another is seen in the efforts of the individual to gain acceptance of his own pre-determined decision by intellectual or emotive arguments. These constitute a form of duplicity in that they are attended by information-seeking and problem-explaining exercises which create the illusion that consultation or participation is taking place. A third manifestation of 'Theory X' is seen in the practice of consulting individuals on the subject of personal implications that might result from a decision made. In this way the support of a majority for an intended decision is amassed by the process of pre-empting hostility on grounds of guaranteed personal safeguards.

A manifestation of 'Theory Y' is seen in the practice of genuine delegation to appropriate sub-groups whose majority decisions are accepted and implemented. The individual who possesses the power to delegate plays no part in the proceedings. An important variant of this is also based on 'Theory Y'. The person with the power to delegate simply identifies the problem for the appropriate group and then participates personally in free discussion until a consensus or majority opinion is established.

A number of models have been created to capture the full range of possibilities indicated above. All of them depend in one form or another upon a two-factor theory (Paisey 1975). The two factors are emphasis on production – the impersonal dimension – and emphasis on morale – the personal dimension. Success turns inevitably upon the blend, but the case for an equal emphasis in *both* has been reinforced by empirically established findings. These include sources as diverse as heavy industry and schools – namely that work output is highest when managerial behaviour has a high equal impact in both dimensions (Misumi and Tasaki 1965; Paisey 1975).

One management style model uses the terms 'job-centred' and 'employee-centred' behaviour and identifies four 'systems' of behaviour in practice (Likert 1961; 1967). *System 1* is authoritarian and coercive. Decisions are made at the top and communication is downward. The 'distance' between superior and subordinate is maximized. *System 2* is authoritative but benevolent with a good deal of subservience. Overt rewards are prominent, there is some delegation and communication is shaped to be received upwards. *System 3* is consultative, also with overt rewards. There are occasional punishments and some involvement in setting objectives and the choice of method. Communications are reciprocal but guarded for upward consumption. *System 4* features participative group management, with wide involvement in setting objectives and choosing methods. Economic rewards are available and communication is free and frank in all directions. Decision-making proceeds on a group basis and there is interlocking membership of groups.

A second model expresses the two factors in terms of 'concern for production' and 'concern for people'. A grid may be formed in which the former is the horizontal axis and the latter the vertical axis. In the 1.1 position lies 'impoverished management', bereft of both concern for people and concern for production. Effective production is unobtainable. People are lazy, apathetic and disengaged. At the interpersonal level, conflict is an ever present threat and relationships are destructive of human personality. In the 1.9 position – low for production, high for people – lies 'country-club management'. The preservation of social solidarity is the overriding consideration even at the expense of production. The confrontation of problems is delayed and escalating difficulties may be concealed beneath a veneer of mutual admiration, excessive familiarity and rationalization.

The opposite extreme to 'country-club management' is that of 'task management' in the 9.1 position, which is high for production, low for people. Human foibles and frailties are dismissed peremptorily in favour of rigid subordination and discipline. People and machines alike are programmed to fit with precision into arrangements which are planned and controlled with inexorable objectivity. The 5.5 position in the middle of the grid represents a management which alternates between giving attention to people and attention to production. This is the 'pendulum management', devoid of conviction and opportunist in style. The ideal is 'team management', which is simultaneously high in concern for production and people. This is the 9.9 position which achieves production with and through people who enjoy their work in a participative structure. It allows the demands of the task and the individual to integrate and to be met simultaneously (Blake and Mouton 1978).

A third model of management style uses the terminology 'task orientation' and 'relationships orientation' to refer to the two factors. Four theoretical styles may be identified: separated; related; dedicated; and integrated. The *separated* category is reserved for individuals who are cautious, careful, conservative and orderly. They appear to prefer paper work, procedures and facts and look for established principles. They are accurate, precise, correct and perfectionist. They are steady, deliberate, patient, calm, modest and discreet. Behaviourally such individuals like to examine, administer, control and maintain. In the *related* category, people are valued and their personal development sought. Individuals in this category appear to be informal, quiet and to go unnoticed. They enjoy long conversations and are sympathetic, approving, accepting, friendly and anxious to create a secure atmosphere for others. In their behaviour they prefer to trust, to listen, to accept, to advise and to encourage.

In the *dedicated* category, individuals are determined, aggressive, confident, busy, driving and initiating. Tasks, responsibilities and standards are conceived at the individual rather than the group level. There is an emphasis on self-reliance, independence and ambition. Rewards, punishments and control are used in a context which stresses the primacy of task. In their behaviour, such people are oriented to organizing, initiating, directing, completing and evaluating. In the *integrated* category, individuals derive their authority from agreed aims, ideals, goals and policies. They value the integration of the individual and the organization and work for participation and low power-differentials. They prefer shared objectives and responsibilities and study the more subtle forms of motivating others to work. Their behavioural pattern is directed towards achieving participation, interaction, motivation, integration and innovation.

In theory, actual organizational members can be grouped into these four categories. In practice they are found to lean either towards being *effective* or *ineffective* in their managerial behaviour. Thus, each of the four theoretical categories finds expression in both 'more effective' and 'less effective' forms. Being 'effective' means adopting behaviour which is correct or adapted to the situation. In other words behaviour that is desirable in one context may be maladaptive in another and, therefore, ineffective (Reddin 1970).

In conclusion, in all these models there is provision for the style which favours building a broader basis of consent, frequent and wide reference to the opinion of others, the involvement of their creative talent, and as full a participation in decision making as practical considerations and the wishes of individuals permit. This style is variously expressed in the models mentioned in this chapter – namely System 4, position 9.9 on the grid and the effective manifestation of the integrated category which is called 'executive style'. This seems to be the cultural adaptation likely to develop still further in the years ahead. It is now being argued that for management at large '... every scenario for business in the eighties shows an increase in the autonomy of people at work, a trend towards consultation, participation, some measure of increased individual involvement'. (Foy 1978:122)

In the case of education in particular it has been concluded that the schools which are generally held to be successful organizations are those in which management involves and stresses consultation, team work and participation. The procedures necessary for this to happen are not concerned to produce *uniformity* but to achieve *unity*. If some members of staff still have reservations about policies and practices which have received substantial support from their colleagues, they rarely withhold active cooperation. Heads recognize that although they are legally accountable for the good order and effectiveness of the school's administration, power-sharing is the best basis for longer term development. The *kind* of leadership given by the head, therefore, is the most important single factor. (Department of Education and Science 1977d:1979)

However, care should be taken to ensure that the essential purposes of the school as an organization are continually borne in mind. Excessive organization maintenance costs are anathema to the realization of the objectives which any organization sets for itself. Hierarchical structures and directive management are economical in this regard but may engender frustration, low morale and disengagement. Participative structures and permissive management incur larger organization maintenance costs but raise morale and effort. Clearly, the beginning of administrative wisdom is to recognize that there is no single and certain way to manage an organization well. Variable circumstances and needs require variable approaches and answers. The manager must constantly exercise judgement about management strategy, and the degree and direction of changes in strategy which are necessary. Wisdom is knowing what to do next.

Summary

The management function in the school as an organization has been shown to include in its wide purview both objective elements and subjective elements. Management is an inescapable function in organization and is a social process for matching objectives and resources. There is a wide variety of styles of management which individuals exhibit, as judged by those with whom they work. These vary in impact on the members of organizations and effect their work output and morale differently.

Discussion topics

1. How far should programmes of initial teacher education and training take account of management concepts and practice?
2. Which management style would you yourself wish to exhibit and wish to see in others?
3. Discuss the following paragraph in the light of this chapter.

> About a third of the schools, including schools of all types and sizes, were very well led. In such schools priorities were clearly defined and included, though with variations in emphasis, the development of pastoral care, close cooperation between academic and pastoral structures, academic success, staff development and appraisal of the school's performance. Most heads in these schools initiated ideas and policy, but also readily encouraged ideas in others and reconciled opposing interests and views. Styles of leadership varied with personality and included both authoritatian and democratic approaches, but most of these heads consulted fully the staff of their schools and allowed decision-making to be widely shared while retaining an overall and acknowledged leadership. Many examples were noted of schools where a group of dedicated senior teachers strongly supported their head teachers, gave leadership to their colleagues in their own right and generated a warm and good humoured atmosphere in the staffroom and throughout the school. (Department of Education and Science 1979:223)

Practical enquiry

Use the model in Fig. 5.1 to analyse the management work of a school of your choice. Ask the head of school to supply examples for each cell in the model.

Ask a range of teachers in each of two contrasting schools to rank in order the decision areas in Fig. 5.2 according to their relative importance for the organization and condition of the school as a whole. Then ask them to identify the participation which they believe they have in each of these decision areas, using the three levels shown in the model. Compare the results for the two schools and discuss the implications of any differences revealed.

6
VIEWPOINTS AND VALUES

Introduction

On many issues, members of the teaching staff of any school are likely to take a similar view. If the school is relatively undisturbed by external pressures, a harmonious and happy working atmosphere is likely to develop. This is the more likely to happen if the school is small and well led, but with good leadership it can also happen in large schools. However, the issues which arise in any school vary in number, complexity and severity. The school's exposure to external influences is great enough in most cases to generate a continual stream of issues. These all have to be faced and a constant process of internal adjustment to the school must be undertaken by its management.

In this case it is probable that different views about a variety of professional issues are to be found among the members of the teaching staff of a school. Sometimes, these views are very strongly held and with a conviction which makes it difficult to achieve a common policy and to carry out an agreed set of practices. This may lead to tension and frustration, which add extra strain to the task of teaching.

Different views may arise quite simply from a misunderstanding or from a lack of information. Provided goodwill exists, misunderstandings can be cleared up if appropriate steps are taken, and the lack of information can be rectified by making the necessary information available. Goodwill, however, does not always exist and it is not uncommon to find that different viewpoints cannot be reconciled easily. Staff may attribute the views of a particular colleague to eccentricity and be able to accommodate them with good humour, especially when a matter of principle is not at stake. When matters of principle *are* at stake it is not easy to shrug off the views of a colleague in such a tolerant way. Differences may persist and generate rancour, leading ultimately to low morale, disengagement and, finally, even schism, as in cases such as the William Tyndale Primary School in London and the Summerhill Secondary School in Scotland in the 1970s.

Schools are not alone in experiencing the constant need to reconcile different viewpoints of principle and practice. It is a commonplace experience in organizations to find that other people do not always take the same view of an event or make the same appraisal of a situation as oneself. This happens even when the event or situation seems perfectly clear and unambiguous in nature. 'The realities which one person experiences seem inescapable to him though they clash with the realities which bind another person.' (Greenfield 1977:92)

When events and situations are complex in nature and difficult to understand, most people are ready to accept differences of view – at least in the initial stage. People often ask one another, 'What do you make of it?', or 'Why do you take this view?', or 'Do you agree with this analysis?' Indeed, 'second opinions' are valued and sometimes raised to virtuous heights in some professions. In organizations, willingness to welcome and engage in the free exchange and appropriation of ideas and practices is the central concept of 'open systems thinking', which many people advocate as vital for the achievement of a happy, healthy and successful organization – particularly in education (Halpin 1966). An organization based on 'open systems thinking' recognizes the existence of different viewpoints and tries to use them as a capital asset for the benefit of the organization – rather than trying to ignore them or hoping they will go away in due course.

The differences of view which teachers exhibit may sometimes be attributed to sheer 'cussedness'. When viewpoints are genuine, and sincerely held, however, it is possible for members to see their own organization and the issues which arise in it in very different ways. They may cling to these different views and still remain devoted to the school, respectively determined to support it in every way they can. Such differences result from the fact that the cognitive abilities and psychological composition of each person are the products of varying congenital and environmental factors. Thus, distinctive viewpoints become characteristic of different individuals.

It is possible, but insensitive, for management to ignore the existence of these characteristic differences of view among organization members as a fundamental condition of 'corporate' or collective effort. To do so is not likely to lead to success. Managerial behaviour is more likely to be successful if two needs are borne in mind. In the first place, a managing teacher must be able to know, to recognize and to take account of the characteristic points of view of those with whom he or she works. Secondly, and of equal importance, a teacher engaged in managing beyond the classroom must surely know and take into account his or her *own* propensities or characteristic points of view.

Different views are based on different values. Insofar as differences become characteristic of the members of an organization they may be regarded as an asset or a hindrance.

This chapter identifies, explains and classifies the various habitual points of view which are found in practice and the premises upon which they are based. The resulting map of these viewpoints shows the range of fundamental positions which teachers take in schools. It shows that characteristically different positions which are taken produce characteristically different responses to the changing circumstances, challenges and reactions which organizational life produces.

An inclusive model has been devised for the purpose. It includes various material from other sources which has been adapted and supplemented. The first part of the model shows how individuals try to understand the organization of which they are members, particularly as a working whole. Individuals are influenced in their perceptions of complex organization by factors in life which are familiar and more immediate to them. Consequently, the human body, human family life and the manifest power and efficiency of machines of all kinds become objects of reference in a person's attempts to comprehend organization as a single entity.

The second part of the model draws on the imagery associated with the familiar experience of travel. It is concerned with how people view the positions which others take. The traveller has a changing relationship with the terrain. At various points on the path a different view of the same scene can be obtained. By analogy, organization members are at different points on the path of their experience in life in general and the organization in which they currently work in particular. Consequently, their views of the organization can be different from one another. This part of the model, therefore, shows how each person tends to view other individuals who are fellow members of the same organization. Significantly different personal viewpoints are identified and their practical outcomes classified.

The third and final part of the model sets out the main areas of personal values and preferences. It is concerned, therefore, with knowing oneself as an organization member and of being able to recognize one's own viewpoint and the fundamental premises upon which that viewpoint is based. The complete model is represented in tabular form at the end of the chapter (Table 6.1).

Understanding the whole school

Understanding anything implies conceptual grasp, which involves the aggregation of many parts into a whole or 'higher integration', and giving the latter some kind of meaning. An organization by definition is a synthesis of elements. An understanding of organization implies an appreciation of the whole and its constituent parts together with its purpose or function.

The human body.   It occasions no surprise that the human body should act as a catalyst in the search for an understanding of the organizational aspects of human life. The first factor that individuals notice is the unitary nature of the body. The second is that the wholeness of the body seems to be more than the sum of the parts. The malfunction or loss of a part is an impairment of the whole, the design of which assumes the indispensability of each part. Every part is different but every part counts. It is the function of each part to perform its characteristic task – no more and no less.

The projection of the body as an aid to achieving an understanding of organization has longstanding antecedents. For example, St Paul wrote to the church he had founded in Corinth: 'There are many different organs, but one body. The eye cannot say to the hand, "I do not need you"; nor the head to the feet, "I do not need you". Quite the contrary: those organs of the body which seem to be more frail than others are indispensable.' (1 Corinthians, Ch. 12)

In the modern age organic theories of organizations echo the principles implicit in such a view. Organization, consisting of many members, like a body, is a developing, adaptive phenomenon. It has increasing 'self-awareness' or 'consciousness' and may assume large powers of self-direction. But its members vary in their ability to make a contribution to the whole. Membership is, therefore, earned and based on merit, since the willingness to contribute varies as well as the ability.

Organizational health is a fluctuating condition and the ill-health of organizational parts sooner or later affects the whole. A 'sick' or malfunctioning member should not be removed, however, but retrained or given therapy in the form of retraining to enable him to resume making a normal and suitable contribution. Surgery in organization, as with the body, is only the last, desperate step.

If these are some of the characteristics of the 'organic' view of organization, it may be said that the perspective adopted is that of competency. In organizational terms, this is a matter of achieving a suitable deployment of differential ability among the organization members so that together a complex task can be undertaken.

> The human body offers a model for the understanding of organization which emphasizes the competency of its members deployed on the basis of differential ability.

The human family. The smallest organization has always been familiar to man in the form of the human family, particularly in its extended form. The salient features of the family are features which may be projected into larger groupings of people or organizations. In the family there is interdependence. Complementary factors are at work. The main feature, however, is the inequality of capacity – physical, intellectual and socio-emotional – of its members.

Parents do not 'choose' their children and offspring do not 'choose' their parents – an arbitrary factor is at work which is coupled with a dependency factor. The notion of authority exists to cope with these related factors. Authority provides support for inadequate parents and helps curb the excesses of rebellious children. The hardness of authority, however, is softened by the simultaneous recognition of the family as a forum of trust, the expression of warmth and the toleration of idiosyncrasies.

The school as an organization is sometimes viewed as a very large family. Its family aspects may be energetically promoted and tenaciously defended. In such cases there would be a strong concern by status-conscious individuals to preserve a paternalistic or maternalistic regime. This in essence provides protection, patronage and reward in return for recognition of authority on the grounds of convention, titles and ranks, but not necessarily merit. The assumption of offices and powers in the organization is derivative in origin. Individuals are expected to be sensitive to their status or positions, and their concomitant authority.

In the school viewed as a family, tasks emanate progressively to larger numbers of people as a result of the decisions of progressively fewer people and, possibly, ultimately one person – the patron or 'father' of the organization – the head of school. The essential characteristic in this case is that of delegation. In the family each member may have particular responsibilities. Typically, as a family grows so the older children are expected to assume greater responsibilities. Delegation assumes a larger vision, greater wisdom and more knowledge on the part of the one person or the few upon whom the many depend for sustenance and inspiration. In operational terms, the organizational emphasis provided by the family as a model is the deployment of formal authority among organization members, by which each is enabled to carry out his or her part of the total work of the organization.

The human family offers a model for the understanding of organization which emphasizes the delegation of responsibilities to its members deployed according to the formal authority they have been given.

The world of nature. Beyond the body and family is the natural environment of one's existence. This, too, provides powerful formative influences. One's perception of the world of nature may lead to a variety of interpretations but the general existence of flora and fauna is an inescapable element of the context of human life and a potential determinant of attitudes.

The ebb and flow or cyclical character of the seasons is an impressive feature. This is the effect of external factors upon plants and animals, shaping the stimuli to which they must respond and providing the basic terms of survival. But within and between the species there is a pattern of existence in terms of their incidence or distribution relative to opportunity.

Many may perceive this as a subtle balance between existing species – the ecological view. This is to emphasize the aspect of overall good order, the total pattern and synthesis which proves to be viable. On the other hand, many perceive the synthesis in terms of the experience of the individual animal or plant involved. This is to emphasize the struggle which the elemental parts of the natural world are inescapably involved in to establish themselves and survive.

In organizations both of these perceptions are expressed in the concept of dominance (Knipe and Maclay 1973). The manifestation of attitudes moulded by this perception would be a deployment of natural power. The dominant ones determine what happens. One might go as far as Hobbes in the *Leviathan* and depict social life without any governmental constraints as 'nasty, brutish and short'. Without the dominant ones, therefore, modern organizations might well become vehicles of unbridled savagery where 'every man's hand is against every man'. When a senior teacher in a London comprehensive school was informed of a television programme which related the hazardous early life of newly-born turtles he commented 'that is how it is for all of us,' as if the dominance order was insufficiently established and defined to prevent continual and arbitrary harassment from all quarters.

On the other hand, the organization might be regarded as an instrument for mitigating the excesses, whilst dealing with the fact, of the struggle for dominance. Organizational life is perforce constantly stimulating. The necessary adjustments of individuals and sub-groups are variously successful. The weaker give way to the stronger and a dominance pattern – however disguised – emerges. This is an irresistible process and precipitates a constant potential for instability – as evident among teachers in their work in schools as anywhere else.

The world of nature offers a model for the understanding of organization which emphasizes the dominance of members deployed according to their natural powers.

The machine. Mechanical devices of all kinds have become commonplace as extensions of the human body's powers for both work and leisure. They generate as much interest as the body itself. The very principles which can so evidently facilitate the invention and use of the machine may be projected for use into other spheres of concern, notably human organization. The characteristics of the machine are demonstrable and normally irrefutable. There can be objectivity, therefore, and agreement, between people over a machine's construction and function. Furthermore, whilst the malfunctioning of one of its parts may reduce the efficiency of the machine sooner or later, each part is more readily and ethically detachable and replaceable than the human body. The authenticity of the function of the machine as a whole and any of its constituent parts can be viewed with unemotional detachment.

In organizations, the attitudes which rely on the efficacy of the machine pay due tribute to the scientific outlook of the modern age. They look to the concept of rationality in organization. Identifiable parts have specific functions and must discharge them or be discarded. Interchangeable parts or flexibility of functions is an important demand. There is a strong emphasis on efficiency – the matching of inputs or resources with output or product. It betrays a skill-conscious or effectiveness-in-action attitude. Skill takes precedence over personality and, therefore, rationality over patronage. Operationally this attitude would result in a deployment of technical tasks, favoured by those in teaching who seek to secure an extensive measure of control over the organization and anathema to those who fear or deplore such attempts at precision.

> The machine offers a model for the understanding of organization which emphasizes rationality among members deployed according to the technical functions to be discharged.

Understanding the viewpoints of others

Organizations loom large in the landscape of human life and have an important bearing on the individual's search for meaning (Frankl 1967). As life, like a journey, proceeds, an accumulation of experiences – some significant, some insignificant – contribute towards the development of an individual's personal view of it. Each new experience in turn acts as an opportunity for either adaptive or maladaptive behaviour. This process may become stressful and it is the concern of many to seek a suitable standpoint which will provide a sense of stability and sanity. An ability to recognize the characteristic viewpoints of others is essential if a senior teacher wishes to work successfully at a managerial level. Some of these are typified as follows. They have been characterized by Furlong (1973) as the Comic View, the Romantic View, the Ironic View and the Tragic View.

Comic view. Those who are persuaded of the efficacy of selected 'gospels' are said to have a comic view of life. The view is comical because it belongs to the pretentious posturings of those who deify a particular cognitive system or philosophical approach as the definitive answer to man's search for meaning and an understanding of the cosmos. Thus the claims of politics, science, technology, behavioural psychology, medicine and similar fields of study when taken in isolation amount to so many entertaining but essentially 'trivial' antics. They are especially regarded as such when they attempt to postulate 'progress' and take a highly abstracted, linear and 'short-cut' view of the complexity of life. There is a constant need to take a whole view and to allow for the basic inability of our finite minds to be able to comprehend the infinite. The comic view *is* comic because there would appear to be an implicit pride and unjustified assurance where none is warranted.

In schools the comic visionary is a person given to the habit of offering mechanistic solutions to all kinds of problems. There is a fondness for precision, prescription and prediction on the basis of a simple conceptualization of cause and effect. There is a love of tidiness and a resistance to muddle. There is a fatal confusion between the intuitive grasp of a complex situation, as may be communicated to others in relatively uncomplicated terms, and the actual implementation of measures which need to be taken as a corrective. The future, it is thought, may be programmed fully and accomplished without delay. No account is taken of the arbitrary and sometimes perverse nature of people in organizations. The uncertainties of school life in particular defy the direct solutions of the comic visionary.

The comic view is that which offers unidimensional explanations of organizational problems

---

Romantic view. In contrast, the romantic view is essentially retrospective rather than prospective. In the experience of those who take a romantic view there exists a perceived reality or condition which exerts a magnetic hold over their emotions. It is inevitably an abstraction, constructed in the image of a unique pattern of personal needs. It represents a perpetual rejection of the *status quo* and an assertion of superiority of view in that the preferred interpretation of the past is in some way specially possessed and understood by the romantic. His attitude of hostility or alienation to the present implies a deprivation which is counterbalanced by the privilege derived from his position of interpreter of a past golden age that can be revived as a solution to the problems of the present.

The romantic visionary in organizations is doctrinaire in the sense that modifications take their cue not from what the situation demands but from what his blue-print demands. It inevitably implies a maladaptive attitude, with a resistance to change, since the criteria chosen for taking and judging action are rooted at worst in prejudice and possibly the recovery of vested interest, previous status and influence. At best they signal the hope of recovery of preferred values which have declined in general esteem.

The romantic view is that which measures present organizational problems against a preferred interpretation of the past.

Ironic view.   The essential element in the make-up of those who take the ironic view is that of detachment, with a resistance to commitment. Psychic energy is derived from not taking oneself or others too seriously. Of course there is the possibility that detachment might mean unconcern or even complacency. Rather than the result of stoical self-discipline, it might appear in practice as a form of self-indulgence akin to aristocratic superiority, facilitated by financial and social security. Detachment could be regarded as the product variously of age – and so of fatigue, of maturity – and so of wisdom, or it could be regarded as being of therapeutic self-analysis – and so of survival strategy (Weekes 1972).

In organizations, the divide between those who seek change for whatever reasons and those who oppose change for whatever reasons often seems unbridgeable. Detachment then appears to parade as conservatism which is interpreted as complacency or indifference. In education this was the case in the 1960s when students in the United States and Western Europe came into confrontation with university administrations. It is the perennial struggle between the imagined 'haves and have-nots' in organizations – whether cast in terms of incomes, participation or advancement.

Teaching as a whole is regarded by some other sectors of employment as being in the grip of those with an ironic view, or detachment, about the shape and condition of life outside the school. A union leader in the United States once said of teachers that one of the prime troubles, if not the chief curse of the teaching profession was that teachers too often took a detached view of the problems that assail society. '… your craft is somewhat above this world of ours; it implies a remoteness from the daily battle of the streets, the neighbourhood and the cities. …' (Quoted by Stinnett 1968:353).

The over-exposure to stimulation and the sanity of detachment are possibilities to which everyone in organizations is subject. The reply to jibes that the ironic view is characteristic of the successful and those who wish to preserve the *status quo* can only be in terms of the obvious. At any given point of time there are certain features of an organization which any one individual *can* change – but a vast number which he *cannot* change. Nowhere is this more true than of teachers in the school, whatever the positions they hold.

> The ironic view is that which urges detachment in coping with organizational problems.

Tragic view.   The essential feature in the tragic view is the recognition that the inescapable human predicament consists of dashed hopes, disappointed faith and unsatisfied yearnings. Yet to make no effort at all is self-destructive – the individual may have to learn to accept an unhappy suspension between mutually disagreeable positions. In making such an effort, however, the individual is exposed to the dangers, terrors and mysteries of the risk in addition to the basic dilemmas of paradox and ambiguity. Those who make the effort are the heroic ones, the tragic figures striving against great odds.

In organizations, the tragic hero is often the awkward individual who seems to delight in attracting hostility and to relish choosing arguments and positions which are bound to generate animosity towards him. It is a lonely stance. If taken by an obscure member of the organization it attracts the limelight to the individual and he can be made into a scapegoat. If taken by the powerful in an organization it rapidly crystallizes opinion. People resent the distant figure at the top and dislike being reminded dramatically of the dilemmas in their own lives.

The individual who takes the tragic view is in constant danger of generating impossible odds to derive a deep satisfaction from non-attainment and self-justification, as if resistant to solutions. Members of organizations need to recognize the virtues of accepting the limitations of reality but of responding courageously to the complexities of existence in organizations at the same time, without turning it into a crusade.

> The tragic view is that which points out the inevitability of failure in dealing with organizational problems

---

Understanding one's own viewpoint

One of the abiding subjects of interest in education is the nature of truth. At some time or other teachers are obliged to consider the question of what is true knowledge and to be concerned that pupils should think about the nature of truth and to value truth. What is truth? The historical question of Pontius Pilate cannot be given an answer with which all would agree.

At the back of a person's views about anything in life there are always some fundamental assumptions. These are clearly of critical importance in any attempt to account for differences of views in the school and in the efforts made to manage it as an organization constructively and effectively. The final part of this chapter is reserved for the identification and description of five critical value systems which are found among teachers. These are called Idealism, Realism, Rationalism, Experimentalism and Existentialism. They are presented in summary form, derived from a number of different sources (Morris 1961; Butler 1966; Bayles 1966; Lawson 1957; Morris 1966; Laing 1967; Hughes 1976; Greenfield 1977).

Idealism. If a person is prone to view objects perceived by the senses as imperfect manifestations of what they *might* be, then that person may be said to be an idealist. The 'might be' here refers to the perfect form of the object which in fact exists not in terms of tangible reality but may do so as an *idea* or *ideal* in the mind of the observer.

All objects, whether inanimate or animate, non-human or human, are considered in relation to the perfected form which can be apprehended and understood by mind alone. Behind all persons, therefore, there is the *idea* of personhood which acts as a reference and touchstone for all thoughts about persons. It actively governs the ways in which an idealist regards a particular person and interacts with him.

For example, a teacher with a grasp of the world of *ideas* would be able to penetrate the 'sensory screen' which surrounds a child and 'see' the ideal which that child might become. To close the gap between the ideal and the actual is impossible by definition, but the possibility of reducing the distance serves as a mainspring for action and judgement.

As far as organizations are concerned, the idealist's position would be that relatively few members of an organization are able to 'see' what an organization as an entity might become. Such people have a drive towards perfection. The alleged possession of the view of the *ideal*, however, does not necessarily imply that the observer has a comprehensive grasp of the existing condition of a particular organization at any point of time. Still less does it imply the capability to correct the composition and course of an organization in accord with that ideal. Above all, however, stands the vexed issue as to whether a vision of the ideal implies any special prescriptive *right* to assume powers to attempt corrective courses of action beyond those attaching to other members of the organization in question.

> Idealism is the tendency to emphasize organization as what it *should* be

Realism. A person persuaded of the importance of natural law does so in the belief in the demonstrable fact that man is himself only part of the cosmos. His powers are strictly finite in a realm of powers which he did not originate and cannot change. The laws which operate in the universe govern all phenomena including the human being and the social predicament. The intelligent way to proceed – and this strategy itself can be seen as a natural law – is to seek to discover the underlying and pervasive laws at work in any prescribed material or human event or series of events.

Man can discover the laws and work with them for his own accommodation. He can work against them only at his peril. Events are 'out there' to be observed. They are neither good nor bad apart from whether or not they are the result of the operations of natural law.

The realist teacher is one inclined to accept what he sees as 'the facts of life' such as the ineradicable differences of ability, interest, potential power and prosperity of individuals. In his organization, the realist will accept what *is* the case rather than emphasize what *might* be the case as the idealist does. He proceeds by way of finding out what is working in practice on the basis of careful observations of the relevant natural laws which permit it to do so. Predictability is the hallmark of realism. There is a drive towards order.

The claim of individuals to be able to discover the natural laws and communicate their findings to others in respect of organizations is as awesome as the claim of idealists to have had a vision of the ideal. Incontestable capability would be omniscience indeed. The natural laws may in fact *in themselves* be absolute, but the frailty and imperfection of human perception, knowing and communicating are 'natural' constraints on any over-weening pretentions of the realist's analysis and correction of organizational ills.

Realism is the tendency to emphasize organization as that which actually exists

---

Rationalism.   Rationalism takes its stand on the claim that the cosmos is a logical construction. The human mind as part of the cosmos is logical in nature and functions as a special means for comprehending the universe. It does so characteristically by intuition – that is, by the immediate and direct action of apprehension.

The facts or truth of a situation are, therefore, self-evident. Once an individual apprehends this by intuition, he or she must then undertake the task of analysis or deductive reasoning, utilizing the logic which is inherent in any question or problem under review as a means for doing so.

In his organizational commitments the rational person looks for the overview or grasp of the whole, supported by a rigorous discipline of analysis for the purpose of elaboration and communication, with rationality in all things. In their views on the curriculum, rationalist teachers are more likely to support well-structured subjects like mathematics than subjects which permit arbitrary structure.

In organizations, the pre-eminence given to logic in both the intellectual and practical spheres predisposes the rationalist to a drive towards making hierarchies. Hierarchy has singularly important implications for the construction and running of organizations. It is self-evident that if the finite powers of man are attempting to cope with the infinite variety of reality, then a rational distribution of effort is needed. Given the purpose, then each person concerned must be assigned a place and responsibility in the organization. One person is logically related to another and retained in position either by self-discipline or externally applied means.

The implicit assumptions of firmness of purpose and stability of organizational arrangements in the rationalist's attitude easily attract charges of vested interest. More seriously, however, in times of rapid change they appear to many to be wilfully maladaptive.

> Rationalism is the tendency to emphasize organization as a matter of logic

Experimentalism. This 'colossus of our age' is also called pragmatism or instrumentalism. Reality to the experimentalist is always in flux. Experience is the only worthwhile measure of reality. This consists of conscious interaction between the human being and other people or objects – all of which are part and parcel of the 'real' world. The experimentalist has a drive towards participation.

Since such experience must inevitably vary from person to person, truth about the cosmos or any part of it must always be temporary, tentative and subject always to 'another view' – itself based upon a different experience. Knowledge is freely made and unmade. It is not fixed and final. Unlike the realist who may feel that consensus is possible in the face of objective 'facts' – that is, the discovery of the natural law and how it operates – the experimentalist stresses the subjective nature of knowledge. It is personal in the sense that it results from individual experience and is the best available knowledge to work with 'until something better comes along'.

The important caveat is that the position taken by an experimentalist is not a pretentious one like that taken by an idealist or a realist. An individual says in effect: 'This is how I find things. I am waiting for the fresh experience of others or myself that will persuade me to change my view.' The experimentalist's position is essentially open to change and, therefore, implies the public nature of knowledge and a free dissemination of views. Knowledge is inevitably a synthesis of views. Though an individual may find a particular synthesis to be disagreeable, it is nonetheless acknowledged as the best knowledge available for the time being.

In organizations an experimentalist proceeds by way of acting on what is known at the present and by studying the consequences of any actions taken. This observation leads to a 'reconstruction of experience'. The individual then uses these consequences as new raw material for the contemplation of further action and a basis for postulating how to implement decisions taken. In the jargon of scientific method, the experimentalist first takes a given situation as a 'problem' because it contains unsatisfactory elements. He then makes an inventory of solutions, including the possible and the improbable and conjectures the consequences of each in turn. In testing the impact made by each by an 'experiment' or 'pilot scheme' he eliminates all but the best which then becomes fully implemented and maintained. Because it works it is 'right' and certainly acceptable to the experimentalist. It is in turn, however, not a final solution but only an interim accommodation.

Experimentalism is the tendency to emphasize organization as a matter of
what works

Existentialism.   The cardinal factor for the existentialist is the absolute
power of choice. Whatever data are assembled and by whatever means
and on whatever subject, the fact remains that each individual for
whatever reasons possesses the inalienable power of choice to accept or
reject them. Individual choice is the ultimate arbiter. No person nor set of
circumstances intrinsically carries an inescapable and superordinate
power to compel conviction and obedience. The drive of the existentialist
is towards diversification.

Being conscious of the fact that he *is* conscious, the existentialist
assumes that he is squarely confronted with an indivisible obligation of
personal responsibility. He cannot 'blame' someone else for his
predicament. Being responsible for one's actions is of the essence. A prior
investigation of the possible consequences of an action before it is taken
is, therefore, an implied requirement in existentialist thinking.

In organizations the existentialist recognizes no authority and no
duty other than those he chooses to recognize. There is no consideration
that he ought to make such recognitions. In a school, for example, the
adoption of educational and resource objectives and professional
performance criteria carries no automatic power to compel his agreement
and support. This is particularly so when the existentialist teacher has
played no part in deciding what they should be. Even if such a teacher
had taken part in deciding what they should be, however, the
existentialist in that teacher could still make it possible for him
subsequently to choose to repudiate the arrangements made. There is no
'moral' duty to stand by them − only a consideration of the consequence
of the particular choice made. However strongly supported a measure
may be, the awesome face of collective decision does not pre-empt his
personal power of choice in the matter.

Existentialism is the tendency to emphasize organization as what members
accept

Summary

Teachers may think about their schools as organizations in very different
ways. When issues arise in schools, they generate different viewpoints,
which are based upon different values of fundamental importance and
priority to the individuals concerned. These can account for very
different assessments of given circumstances and will lead to different

preferences as solutions to the same problem. Those who occupy positions of managerial importance are included in this – they too have particular and characteristic views of reality. Organization must inevitably accommodate these differences in one way or another. Differences of view and different values may be regarded as a hindrance or as an asset in the management of organization.

A number of ways of trying to understand what organizations are like as entities, the view one may take of the viewpoints of others, and the values which affect one's own views, are indentified and described. These are embodied in an inclusive model, summarized as Table 6.1.

Table 6.1 Inclusive model of viewpoints and values

Understanding the whole school		
Viewpoint	*Value*	*Organizational outcome*
Human body	Competency	Deployment of differential ability
Human family	Delegation	Deployment of formal authority
World of nature	Dominance	Deployment of natural power
The machine	Rationality	Deployment of technical tasks
Understanding the viewpoints of others		
Viewpoint	*Value*	*Organizational outcome*
Comic view	Definitive Explanations	Resistance to muddle
Romantic view	Recovery of former state	Resistance to change
Ironic view	Detachment	Resistance to commitment
Tragic view	Inevitable paradox	Resistance to solutions
Understanding one's own viewpoint		
Viewpoint	*Value*	*Organizational outcome*
Idealism	Mental process	Drive towards perfection
Realism	Natural law	Drive towards order
Rationalism	Intuition	Drive towards hierarchy
Experimentalism	Experience	Drive towards participation
Existentialism	Choice	Drive towards diversification

Discussion topics

1. Discuss the feasibility and desirability of having a teaching staff which takes a similar view of organization. Is the chance of compatible views and values equally likely to occur in primary schools and secondary schools?

2. Discuss the likelihood of a correlation in teaching between one's own academic discipline and regular teaching work on the one hand, and one's way of thinking about organization on the other.

Practical enquiry

1. Take notes of the contributions of different speakers at a meeting of

teaching staff in a school. Identify the characteristic ways of thinking about the school which they represent and discuss the degree of consistency or eclecticism which each shows.

2. Discuss with (a) a young teacher and (b) the head of the same school (or other senior member of staff) the way that each thinks about his or her school as an organization.

BIBLIOGRAPHY

Ader, J. (1975) *Building Implications of the Multi-Option School*, OECD, Paris.

Adair, J. (1979) *Training for Leadership*, Gower Press, Farnborough, Hampshire.

Albert, J. G. (1974) Wanted: experiments in reducing the cost of education, *Phi Delta Kappan*, **LV**(7) March, pp. 444–5.

Allen, I. *et al.* (1975) *Working an Integrated Day*, Ward Lock, London.

Alutto, J. A. and **Belasco, J. A.** (1972) A typology for participation in organizational decision making, *Administrative Science Quarterly*, **17**(1), March, pp. 117–25.

Ammerman, H. and **Melching, W.** (1966) *The Derivation, Analysis and Classification of Instructional Objectives*, HumRRO Technical Report 66–4, May, George Washington University, Alexandria, Virginia.

Anstis, G. M. (1967) School is a living organism, Ch. 8, pp. 47–51, in Clegg, Sir A. *et al.*, *The Middle School; a Symposium*, The Schoolmaster Publishing Company, Kettering.

Ardrey, R. (1972) *The Social Contract*, Fontana, London.

Argyle, M. (1958) Supervisory methods related to productivity, absenteeism and labour turnover, *Human Relations*, **11**(1), pp. 23–40.

Argyris, C. (1960) *Understanding Organizational Behaviour*, Tavistock, London.

Ashby, E. (1966) *Technology and the Academics*, Macmillan, London.

Ashton, P., Kneen, P. and **Davies, F.** (1975) *Aims into Practice in the Primary School*, University of London Press, London.

Bamber, C. (1979) *Student and Teacher Absenteeism*, Phi Delta Kappa, Bloomington, Indiana.

Bardo, P. (1979) The pain of teacher burnout: a case history, *Phi Delta Kappan*, **61**(1), December, pp. 252–4.

Barnard, C. I. (1964) *The Functions of the Executive*, Harvard University Press, Cambridge, Massachusetts.

Barry, C. H. and **Tye, F.** (1972) *Running a School*, Temple Smith, London.

Bayles, E. E. (1966) *Pragmatism in Education*, Harper and Row, New York.

Berger, C. (1978) Teaching science, *Practical Applications of Research*, Phi Delta Kappa, **1**(1), September.

Bennett, S. J. (1974) *The School: an Organizational Analysis*, Blackie, London.

Berkshire County Council (1979a) *Accounting Manual*, Berkshire County Council, Reading.

Berkshire County Council (1979b) *County Primary, Nursery, Special and Secondary Schools: Rules of Management/Articles of Government*, Berkshire County Council, Reading.

Berkshire Education Committee (1978) *Guide to Links between Schools and Industry in Berkshire*, Berkshire Education Committee, Reading.

Berkshire Education Committee (1979) *Headteachers' Handbook*, Berkshire Education Committee, Reading.

Bernstein, B. (1967) Open schools, open society, *New Society*, 14 September.

Bernstein, B., Elvin, H. L. and **Peters, R. S.** (1966) Ritual in education, *Philosophical Transactions of the Royal Society of London*, Series B, **251**(772), pp. 429–36.

Bidwell, C. E. (1965) The school as a formal organization, **Ch. 23**, pp. 972–1022 in March, J. G. (ed.), *Handbook of Organizations*, Rand McNally, Chicago.

Bion, W. R. (1961) *Experiences in Groups*, Tavistock, London.

Blake, R. R. and **Mouton, J. S.** (1978) *The New Managerial Grid*, Gulf, Houston.

Blau, P. M. (1956) *Bureaucracy in Modern Society*, Random House, New York.

Blau, P. M. and **Schoenherr, R. A.** (1971) *The Structure of Organization*, Basic Books, New York.

Blaug, M. (1972) *An Introduction to the Economics of Education*, Penguin, Harmondsworth.

Bloch, A. (1978) Combat neurosis in inner city schools, *American Journal of Psychiatry*, October.

Bloom, B. S. (1980) The new direction in educational research: alterable variables, *Phi Delta Kappan*, **61**(6), February, pp. 382–5.

Blyth, W. A. L. and **Derricott, R.** (1977) *The Social Significance of Middle Schools*, Batsford, London.

Boulding, K. E. (1953) *The Organizational Revolution*, Harper and Row, New York.

Briault, E. (1974) *Allocation and Management of Resources in Schools*, Council for Educational Technology for the United Kingdom, London.

British Medical Association (1979) *The BMA Book of Executive Health*, Times Books and The British Medical Association, London.

Brodie, M. (1979) *Teachers – Reluctant Managers?*, Thames Valley Regional Management Centre, Slough.

Brodinsky, B. (1979) Something happened: education in the seventies, *Phi Delta Kappan*, **61**(4), December, pp. 238–41.

Brooksbank, K. (1972) Management, organisation and discipline, **Ch. 1**, pp. 9–12, in National Association of Schoolmasters, Special Report, *Management, Organisation and Discipline*, Hemel Hempstead.

Burgess, T. (1979) Ways to learn, *Journal of the Association of Colleges Implementing Diploma in Higher Education Programmes*, **2**(2), July, pp. 39–48.

Burns, T. and **Stalker, G. M.** (1968) *The Management of Innovation*, Tavistock, London.

Burrows, J. (1978) *The Middle School; High Road or Dead End?*, Woburn Press, London.

Butler, J. D. (1966) *Idealism in Education*, Harper and Row, New York.

Cartwright, D. (1965) Influence, leadership, control, **Ch. 1**, pp. 1–47 in

March, J. G. (ed.), *Handbook of Organizations*, Rand McNally, Chicago.

Child, J. (1977) *Organization – a Guide to Problems and Practice*, Harper and Row, London.

Churchman, C. W. (1969) *The Systems Approach*, Delta, New York.

Clegg, Sir A. (1974) Much to worry us, *The Times Educational Supplement*, 11 October.

Coleman, J. (1966) *Equality of Educational Opportunity*, National Centre for Educational Statistics, Washington, DC.

Coleman, V. (1976) *Stress Control*, Eurostates Marketing, London.

Cooper, C. and **Marshall, J.** (1978) *Understanding Executive Stress*, Macmillan, London.

Cyert, R. M. and **March, J. G.** (1963) *A Behavioral Theory of the Firm*, Prentice-Hall, Englewood Cliffs, New Jersey.

Dale, E. (1969) *Audio-Visual Methods in Teaching*, Holt, Rinehart and Winston, New York.

Davies, I. K. (1976) *Objectives in Curriculum Design*, McGraw-Hill, New York.

Department of Education and Science (1965) *Circular 10/65*, London.

Department of Education and Science (1970) *HMI Today and Tomorrow*, London.

Department of Education and Science (1977a) *A New Partnership for our Schools*, Report of the Committee of Enquiry, Chairman, Mr Tom Taylor, HMSO, London.

Department of Education and Science (1977b) *Curriculum 11–16*, London.

Department of Education and Science (1977c) *Education in Schools*, Government Green Paper, HMSO, London.

Department of Education and Science (1977d) *Ten Good Schools*, HMSO, London.

Department of Education and Science (1978) *Primary Education in England*, HMSO, London.

Department of Education and Science (1979) *Aspects of Secondary Education in England – A Survey by H.M. Inspectors of Schools*, HMSO, London.

Dewey, J. (1937) *Democracy and Educational Administration*, Official Report, New Orleans Convention, The American Association of School Administrators, National Educational Association, Washington, DC.

Donaldson, P. R. (1970) *Role Expectations of Primary School Headteachers*, Unpublished Dissertation for the Diploma in Child Development, University of London.

Dreeben, R. (1973) The school as a workplace, **Ch. 14**, pp. 450–73, in Travers, R. (ed.), *Second Handbook of Research on Teaching*, Rand McNally, Chicago.

Drucker, P. (1962) *The New Society*, Harper and Row, New York.

Drucker, P. F. (1964) *Managing for Results*, Harper and Row, New York.

Drucker, P. F. (1966) *The Effective Executive*, Harper and Row, New York.

Dunham, J. (1978) Change and stress in the head of department's role, *Educational Research*, **21**(1), pp. 44–7.

Dunham, J. (1979) *Organizational Stress in Schools*, unpublished paper, University of Bath.

Dunsire, A. (1979) *Administration – the Word and the Science*, Martin Robertson, Oxford.

Education (1979) The secondary school survey, *Digest*, Vol. 154, No. 23, 7

December, pp. i–iv.

Emmett, D. (1967) *Rules, Roles and Relations*, Macmillan, London.

Etzioni, A. (1961) *A Comparative Analysis of Complex Organizations*, Free Press, Glencoe, Illinois.

Etzioni, A. (1964) *Modern Organizations*, Prentice-Hall, Englewood Cliffs, New Jersey.

Featherstone, J. (1974) Measuring what schools achieve, *Phi Delta Kappan*, LV(7), March, pp. 448–50.

Fiedler, F. E. (1965) Engineer the job to fit the manager, *Harvard Business Review*, 43(5), September–October, pp. 115–22.

Fiedler, F. E. (1967) *A Theory of Leadership Effectiveness*, McGraw-Hill, New York.

Forsythe, E. (1978) *A Less Anxious You: Coping with Anxiety in the Modern World*, Luscombe, London.

Forward, R. W. (1971) *Teaching Together*, Themes in Education, No. 27, University of Exeter, Institute of Education, Exeter.

Foy, N. (1978) *The Missing Links: British Management Education in the Eighties*, Oxford Centre for Management Studies, Oxford.

Frankl, V. E. (1967) *Psychotherapy and Existentialism*, Simon and Schuster, New York.

Freeman, J. (1979) The joy of teaching: another case history, *Phi Delta Kappan*, 61(1), December, pp. 254–6.

Furlong, M. (1973) *The End of our Exploring*, Hodder and Stoughton, London.

Gagné, R. M. and **Briggs, L. J.** (1979) *Principles of Instructional Design*, Holt, Rinehart and Winston, New York.

Galbraith, J. R. (1977) *Organization Design*, Addison-Wesley, Reading, Massachusetts.

Gannon, T. and **Whalley, A.** (1975) *Middle Schools*, Heinemann, London.

Geddes, N. (ed.) (1973) *Primary School Handbook*, Macmillan, London.

Glatter, R. (1973) Off-the-job staff development in education, pp. 11–20, in Pratt, S. (ed.), *Staff Development in Education*, Councils and Education Press, London.

Glatter, R. (1976) Staff development in and out of school, *Secondary Education*, 6(2), November, pp. 3–5.

Goble, N. M. and **Porter, J. F.** (1977) *The Changing Role of the Teacher*, UNESCO, Paris.

Goffman, E. (1970) *Asylums*, Pelican, Harmondsworth.

Golembiewski, R. T. (1965) Small groups and large organizations, **Ch. 3**, pp. 87–141, in March, J. G. (ed.), *Handbook of Organizations*, Rand McNally, Chicago.

Gouldner, A. W. (1955) *Patterns of Industrial Democracy*, Routledge and Kegan Paul, London.

Gray, H. L. (1979a) *Change and Management in Schools*, Nafferton Books, Driffield.

Gray, H. L. (1979b) *The School as an Organization*, Nafferton Books, Driffield.

Great Britain, The Department of Trade (1977) *Report of the Committee of Enquiry on Industrial Democracy*, Cmnd. 6706, Chairman, Lord Bullock, HMSO, London.

Greenfield, T. B. (1977) Where does self belong in the study of organizations? Response to a symposium, *Educational Administration*, 6(1), Winter, pp. 81–101.

Guilford, J. P. (1959) Three faces of intellect, *American Psychologist*, **14**(8), August, pp. 469–79.

Hacon, R. (1961) *Management Training: Aims and Methods*, English Universities Press, London.

Halpin, A. W. (1966) *Theory and Research in Administration*, Macmillan, New York.

Halpin, A. W. (1967) *Administrative Theory in Education*, Macmillan, New York.

Hampshire Education Committee (1976) *County Secondary Schools and Secondary Colleges: Instrument of Government and Articles of Government*, Hampshire County Council, Winchester.

Hampshire Education Committee (1977) *County Primary Schools: Instrument of Management and Rules of Management*, Hampshire County Council, Winchester.

Hampshire Education Committee (1979) *North West Hampshire: Administrative Handbook*, Hampshire Education Committee, Winchester.

Handy, C. B. (1976) *Understanding Organizations*, Penguin, Harmondsworth.

Harlen, W., Darwin, Sr. A. and **Murphy, M.** (1977) *Introducing Match and Mismatch*, Progress in Learning Science, A Schools Council Project, Schools Council, University of Reading, Reading.

Harlen, W. (ed.)(1978) *Evaluation and the Teacher's Role*, Macmillan, London.

Headmasters' Association (1972) *The Government of Schools*, London.

Henley Mercury (1979), Thursday, 14 June.

Herzberg, F. (1966) *Work and the Nature of Man*, World Publishing Company, New York.

Hicks, H. G. (1972) *The Management of Organizations: a Systems and Human Resources Approach*, McGraw-Hill, New York.

Hilsum, S. and **Cane, B.** (1971) *The Teacher's Day*, National Foundation for Educational Research, Slough.

Hirst, P. H. and **Peters, R. S.** (1970) *The Logic of Education*, Routledge and Kegan Paul, London.

Homans, G. C. (1961) *Social Behaviour*, Routledge and Kegan Paul, London.

Howard, A. W. (1968) *Teaching in Middle Schools*, International Textbook Company, New York.

Howells, G. W. (1972) *Executive Aspects of Man Management*, Pitman, London.

Hughes, M. G. (ed.)(1974) *Secondary School Administration*, Pergamon, Oxford.

Hughes, M. G. (ed.)(1975) *Administering Education: International Challenge*, Athlone Press, London.

Hughes, M. G. (ed.)(1976) Barr Greenfield and organization theory: a symposium, *Educational Administration*, **5**(1), Autumn, pp. 1–13.

Illich, I. (1973) *Deschooling Society*, Penguin, Harmondsworth.

Inner London Education Authority (1977) *School Governors' Handbook*, London.

International Labour Office (1964)(1978) *Introduction to Work Study*, Geneva.

Isle of Thanet Gazette (1979) Friday, 13 July.

Isle of Thanet Gazette (1980) Friday, 7 March.

Jackson, K. (1975) *The Art of Solving Problems*, Heinemann, London.
James, E. (1949) *An Essay on the Content of Education*, Harrap, London.
. Jarman, C. (1977) A survival kit for children transferring to secondary school, *Where*, 124, January, pp. 4–5.
Jencks, C. *et al.* (1973) *Inequality: A Reassessment of the Effect of Family and Schooling in America*, Allen Lane, London.
Jennings, A. (1975) The participation of the teaching staff in decision-making in schools, pp. 24–40, in Andrews, P. and Parkes, D. (eds.) Participation, Accountability and Decision-Making at Institutional Level, *Proceedings of the Third Annual Conference of the British Educational Administration Society*, Spring, British Educational Administration Society, Coombe Lodge, Blagdon, Bristol.
Jennings, A. (ed.) (1977) *Management and Headship in the Secondary School*, Ward Lock, London.
Johnson, R. A., Kast, F. E. and Rosenzweig, J. E. (1967) *The Theory and Management of Systems*, McGraw-Hill, New York.
Judge, H. (1974) Plea to lift monopoly in schooling, *The Times Educational Supplement*, 6 September, London.
Judge, H. (1974) *School is Not Yet Dead*, Longman, London.
Kahn, R. L. *et al.* (1964) *Organizational Stress: Studies in Role Conflict and Ambiguity*, Wiley, New York.
Kaufman, R. (1976) *Identifying and Solving Problems: A System Approach*, University Associates, La Jolla, California.
Kingdon, D. R. (1973) *Matrix Organization*, Tavistock, London.
Klaus, D. J. and Glaser, R. (1960) *Increasing Team Proficiency through Training: A Program of Research*, American Institute for Research, Pittsburgh.
Knipe, H. and Maclay, G. (1973) *The Dominant Man*, Fontana, London.
Koerner, J. D. (1968) *Reform in Education: England and the United States*, Weidenfeld and Nicolson, New York.
Krathwohl, D. R. (1965) Stating objectives appropriately for programme, for curriculum and for instructional materials development, *Journal of Teacher Education*, 16, March.
Kynaston Reeves, T. (1967) Constrained and facilitated behaviour: a typology of behaviour in economic organizations, *British Journal of Industrial Relations*, 5(2), July, pp. 145–61.
Laing, R. D. (1967) *The Politics of Experience*, Penguin, Harmondsworth.
Lambert, K. (1979) Size of school and other factors in school organisation: the influence of perceptions in large school theory, *Educational Administration*, 7(2), Summer, pp. 74–98.
Langley County Secondary School (1979) *A Handbook for Parents and Pupils*, Slough.
Lawler, E. E. (1969) Job design and employee motivation, *Personnel Psychology*, XXII.
Lawson, W. (1957) Neo-Thomism, Ch. 2, pp. 43–59 in Judges, A. V. (ed.) *Education and the Philosophic Mind*, Harrap, London.
Leavitt, H. J. (1965) Applied organizational change in industry: structural, technological and humanistic approaches, Ch. 27, pp. 1144–70 in March, J. G. (ed.) *Handbook of Organizations*, Rand McNally, Chicago.
Le Courrier (1975) Bulletin d'Information du Ministère, 10, 26 Mai, Paris.
Lieberman, M. (1956) *Education as a Profession*, Prentice-Hall, Englewood Cliffs, New Jersey.

Lieberman, M. (1970) An overview of accountability, *Phi Delta Kappan*, **LII**(4), December, pp. 194–5.
Light, A. J. (1973) Staff development in education – the search for a strategy, pp. 5–10 in Pratt, S. (ed.) *Staff Development in Education*, Councils and Education Press, London.
Likert, R. (1961) *New Patterns of Management*, McGraw-Hill, New York.
Likert, R. (1967) *The Human Organization: Its Management and Value*, McGraw-Hill, New York.
Lockyer, K. G. (1962) *Factory Management*, Pitman, London.
Lortie, D. C. (1973) Observations on teaching as work, **Ch. 15**, pp. 474–97 in Travers, R. (ed.) *Second Handbook of Research on Teaching*, Rand McNally, Chicago.
Lovell, K. (1967) *Team Teaching*, University of Leeds Institute of Education, Leeds.
Lyons, G. (1976) *Heads' Tasks*, National Foundation for Educational Research, Slough.
Lyons, T. P. (1971) *The Personnel Function in a Changing Environment*, Pitman, London.
Maclure, S. (1974) The writing on the wall, *The Times Educational Supplement*, London, 26 July.
Mager, R. F. (1962) *Preparing Instructional Objectives*, Fearon, Palo Alto, California.
Marshall, J. and **Cooper, C. L.** (1979) *Executives under Pressure: A Psychological Study*, Macmillan, London.
Mayo, E. (1949) *The Social Problems of an Industrial Civilization*, Routledge and Kegan Paul, London.
Melhuish, A. (1978) *Executive Health*, Business Books, London.
Meredith, P. (1974) A century of regression, *Forum*, **16**(2), Spring, pp. 36–9.
McAshan, H. H. (1970) *Writing Behavioral Objectives, A New Approach*, Harper and Row, New York.
McGregor, D. (1960) *The Human Side of Enterprise*, McGraw-Hill, New York.
McGregor, D. (1967) *The Professional Manager*, McGraw-Hill, New York.
Miles, R. E. (1971) Human Relations or Human Resources?, pp. 229–40 in Kolb, D. A., Rubin, I. M. and McIntyre, J. M. (eds.), *Organizational Psychology*, Prentice-Hall, Englewood Cliffs, New Jersey.
Miles, R. E. (1975) *Theories of Management: Implications for Organizational Behavior and Development*, McGraw-Hill, Kogakusha, Tokyo.
Milgram, S. (1974) *Obedience to Authority*, Tavistock, London.
Miller, R. B. (1962) Task description and analysis, **Ch. 6**, pp. 187–228 in Gagné, R. M. (ed.) *Psychological Principles in System Development*, Holt, Rinehart and Winston, New York.
Misumi, J. and **Tasaki, T.** (1965) A study on the effectiveness of supervisory patterns in a Japanese hierarchical organization, *Japanese Psychological Review*, **7**(4), December, pp. 151–62.
Morris, V. C. (1961) *Philosophy and the American School*, Houghton Mifflin, Boston.
Morris, V. C. (1966) *Existentialism in Education*, Harper and Row, New York.
Nash, P., Kazamias, A. M. and **Perkinson, H. J.** (eds.) (1967) *The Educated Man: Studies in the History of Educational Thought*, Wiley, New York.

National Association of Schoolmasters (1972) *Management, Organization and Discipline*, Hemel Hempstead.

National Association of Schoolmasters/Union of Women Teachers (1976) *Stress in Schools*, Hemel Hempstead.

National Association of Youth Service Officers (1974) *Introduction*, Programme for the Third Annual Regional Conference, The Youth and Community Service and the School, held at Oxford, 29 November.

National Union of Teachers (1973) *Teacher Participation: An Executive Report*, London.

Newman, D. (1973) *Organization Design*, Arnold, London.

Nyström, H. (1979) *Creativity and Innovation*, Wiley, NAn Introduction to the Philosophy of Education, Routledge and Kegan Paul, London.

Olivero, J. L. (1970) The meaning and application of differentiated staffing in teaching, *Phi Delta Kapparr*, LII(1), September, pp. 36–40.

Owens, R. G. (1970) *Organizational Behavior in Schools*, Prentice-Hall, Englewood Cliffs, New Jersey.

Oxfordshire County Council (1979) *Starting Points in Self Evaluation*, Oxfordshire Education Department, Oxford.

Packwood, T. (1977) The school as a hierarchy, *Educational Administration*, 5(2), Spring, pp. 1–6.

Paisey, A. (1981) *Small Organizations – The Management of Primary and Middle Schools*, National Foundation for Educational Research, Slough.

Paisey, A. H. and **Paisey, T. J.** (1980) The question of style in educational management, *Educational Administration*. 9(1), Autumn, pp. 95–106.

Paisey, H.A.G. (1975) *The Behavioural Strategy of Teachers in Britain and the United States*, National Foundation for Educational Research, Slough.

Pellegrin, R. J. (1976) Schools as work settings, **Ch. 8**, pp. 343–74, in Dubin, R. (ed.) *Handbook of Work, Organization, and Society*, Rand McNally, Chicago.

Perrow, C. (1974) *Organizational Analysis – A Sociological View*, Tavistock, London.

Peters, R. S. (1966) *Ethics and Education*, Allen and Unwin, London.

Peters, R. S. (ed.)(1976) *The Role of the Head*, Routledge and Kegan Paul, London.

Phi Delta Kappa (1979) *Guidelines for the Effective Incorporation of Parents into the Instructional Process*, Bloomington, Indiana.

Popper, S. H. (1967) *The American Middle School: An Organizational Analysis*, Blaisdell, Waltham, Massachusetts.

Poster, C. (1976) *School Decision Making*, Heinemann, London.

Postman, N. and **Weingartner, C.** (1973) *How to Recognize a Good School*, Phi Delta Kappa, Bloomington, Indiana.

Prior, P. J. (1977) *Leadership is not a Bowler Hat*, David and Charles, Newton Abbot, Devon.

Pugh, D. S. (ed.)(1971) *Organization Theory*, Penguin, Harmondsworth.

Pugh, D. S., Hickson, D. J. and **Hinings, C. R.** (1974) *Writers on Organizations*, Penguin, Harmondsworth.

Pugh, D. S. and **Hickson, D. J.** (1976) *Organizational Structure in its Context: Aston Programme 1*, Saxon House, London.

Pugh, D. S. and **Hinings, C. R.** (1976) *Organizational Structure: Extensions and Replications*, Saxon House, London.

Reading Chronicle (1979) Friday, 13 July.

Reddin, W. J. (1970) *Managerial Effectiveness*, McGraw-Hill, New York.

Reuchlin, M. (1964) *Pupil Guidance, Facts and Problems*, Council for Cultural Cooperation of the Council of Europe, Strasbourg.

Richardson, E. (1973) *The Teacher, the School and the Task of Management*, Heinemann, London.

Ridgway, L. (1976) *Task of the Teacher in the Primary School*, Ward Lock, London.

Riggs, F. W. (1957) Agraria and industria – towards a typology of comparative administration, in Giffin, W. J. (ed.) *Towards the Comparative Study of Public Administration*, Indiana University Press, Bloomington, Indiana.

Rintoul, K. and **Thorne, K.** (1975) *Open Plan Organization in the Primary School*, Ward Lock, London.

Robinson, D. W. (1974) Is this the right approach to student rights? *Phi Delta Kappan*, LVI(4), December, pp. 234–6.

Rockwell, W. F. (1968) The eight hats of the executive, *Ambassador*, Trans-World Airways, Minnesota, July–August.

Romiszowski, A. J. (1970) *The Systems Approach to Education and Training*, Kogan Page, London.

Rutter, M. *et al.* (1979) *Fifteen Thousand Hours: Secondary Schools and their Effects on Children*, Harvard University Press, Cambridge, Massachusetts.

Schon, D. (1971) *Beyond the Stable State*, Temple Smith, London.

Shane, H. G. (1973) *The Educational Significance of the Future*, Phi Delta Kappa, Bloomington, Indiana.

Sharma, C. L. (1963) *A Comparative Study of the Processes of Making and Taking Decisions within Schools in the U.K. and U.S.A.*, unpublished Ph.D. Thesis, University of London.

Shepard, H. A. (1965) Changing interpersonal and intergroup relationships in organizations, **Ch. 26,** pp. 1115–43, in March, J. G. (ed.) *Handbook of Organizations*, Rand McNally, Chicago.

Sim, M. (1970) *Tutors and their Students*, Livingstone, London.

Simmons, D. D. (1971) Management styles, REA, 14–121, 1–4, in Simmons, D. D. (ed.) *College Management – Readings and Cases*, **1**, The Further Education Staff College, Coombe Lodge, Blagdon, Bristol.

Simon, H. A. (1949) *Administrative Behavior*, Macmillan, New York.

Simon, H. A. (1960) *The New Science of Management Decision*, Harper and Row, New York.

Society of Education Officers (1974) *Management in the Education Service: Challenge and Response*, Councils and Education Press, London.

St Edward's School (1979) *Development Appeal*, Oxford.

Steinman, M. (1974) as reported in *The Times Educational Supplement*, London, 26 April.

Stewart, R. (1967) *Managers and their Jobs*, McGraw-Hill, New York.

Stewart, R. (1976) *Contrasts in Management*, McGraw-Hill, New York.

Stinnett, T. M. (1968) Teacher professionalization: challenge and promise, **Part V,** pp. 352–9 in Havighurst, R. J. *et al.* (eds.) *Society and Education*, Allyn and Bacon, Boston.

Sun (1979) Friday, 13 July.

Taylor, B. (1975) Comparison between types of institution in an LEA, pp. 3–11, in Andrews, P. and Parkes, D, (eds.). Participation, accountability and decision-making at institutional level, *Proceedings of the*

Third Annual Conference of the British Educational Administration Society, Spring.

Taylor, F. W. (1947) *Scientific Management*, Harper and Row, London.

The Daily Telegraph (1979) Saturday, 19 May.

The Greneway School (1974) *Handbook for Parents*, Royston, Herts.

The Henley Standard (1979a) Friday, 6 April.

The Henley Standard (1979b) Friday, 20 July.

The Henley Standard (1979c) Friday, 24 August.

The Henley Standard (1979d) Thursday, 14 December.

The House of Commons (1977) *Tenth Report from the Expenditure Committee*: The Attainments of the School Leaver, HMSO, London.

Thomas, S. (1980) What makes teachers tired?, *The Guardian*, Tuesday, 11 March.

Thompson, J. D. (1967) *Organizations in Action*, McGraw-Hill, New York.

Thornbury, R., Gillespie, J. and **Wilkinson, G.** (1979) *Resource Organization in Secondary Schools: Report of an Investigation*, Council for Educational Technology, London.

Turner, C. (1977) Organizing educational institutions as anarchies, *Educational Administration*, 5(2), Spring, pp. 6–12.

Turner, C. M. (1974) The head teacher as manager, *Journal of Educational Administration and History*, 6(2), July.

Tyler, R. W. (1967) The knowledge explosion; implications for secondary education in Full, H. (ed.), Part 2, pp. 106–14, *Controversy in American Education: An Anthology of Crucial Issues*, Macmillan, New York.

Urwick, L. (1963) *The Elements of Administration*, Pitman, London.

Vaizey, J. (1974) Personal column, *The Times Educational Supplement*, London, 26 February.

Walsh, D. (1979) Classroom stress and teacher burnout, *Phi Delta Kappan*, 61(4), December, p. 253.

Walton, J. (ed.) (1971) *The Integrated Day in Theory and Practice*, Ward Lock, London.

Watts, A. G. (1974) Teaching decision making, *The Times Educational Supplement*, 8 March.

Watts, J. (1976) Sharing it out: the role of the head in participatory government, **Ch. 7**, pp. 127–36, in Peters, R. S. (ed.), *The Role of the Head*, Routledge and Kegan Paul, London.

Weekes, C. (1972) *Peace from Nervous Suffering*, Angus and Robertson, London.

Westwood Farm County Junior School (1976) *Handbook to Parents*, Reading, Berkshire.

Wheeler, G. E. (1971) Organisational stress, Commentary on the case study 'A Head of His Time', ORG 14–100(3) pp. 1–4, in Simmons, D. D. (ed.) *College Management – Readings and Cases*, 1, The Further Education Staff College, Coombe Lodge, Blagdon, Bristol.

Woolfolk, R. L. and **Richardson, F. C.** (1979) *Stress, Sanity and Survival*, Futura, London.

Wright, B. (1975) *Executive Ease and Disease*, Gower, London.

Wyant, T. G. (1971) *Systems Thinking*, unpublished, Coventry College of Technology.

Zaleznik, A. (1965) Interpersonal relations in organizations, **Ch. 13**, pp. 574–613, in March, J. G. (ed.), *Handbook of Organizations*, Rand

McNally, Chicago.

Zimmerman, W. G. (1974) Human rights and administrative responsibility, *Phi Delta Kappan*, 56(4), December, pp. 243 and 247.

INDEX